INDIAN SUMMER

INDIAN SUMMER

Traditional Life among the
Choinumne Indians of California's
San Joaquin Valley

Thomas Jefferson Mayfield

Introduction by Malcolm Margolin

Heyday Books, Berkeley, California
Great Valley Books

Library of Congress Cataloging-in-Publication Data
Mayfield, Thomas Jefferson, ca. 1843-1928
Indian summer : traditional life among the Choinumne Indians of California's San Joaquin Valley / by Thomas Jefferson Mayfield ; introduction by Malcolm Margolin.
p. cm.
Reprint of work first copyrighted 1929.
Includes index.
ISBN 0-930588-64-9

1. Mayfield, Thomas Jefferson, ca. 1843-1928. 2. Yokuts Indians–Social life and customs. 3. California–History–1850-1950. I. Title.
E99.Y75M39 1993   979.4'004974
            QBI93-21812

Cover Art: Carl Dennis Buell
Printing and Binding: McNaughton & Gunn, Saline MI

Orders, inquiries, and correspondence should be addressed to:
    Heyday Books
    P. O. Box 9145, Berkeley, CA 94709
    (510) 549-3564, Fax (510) 549-1889
    www.heydaybooks.com

Printed in the United States of America

10 9 8 7 6 5 4 3 2

Acknowledgements

I am very grateful to:

—Monna Latta Olson for permission to use material from *Uncle Jeff's Story* and *Tailholt Tales*.

—Lillian Vallee, whose enthusiasm for the Central Valley and its history led me to find this text.

—Craig Bates, curator, and Linda Eade, librarian, at the Yosemite National Park Museum and Research Library for their help in acquiring photos and gaining access to the Latta archives.

—Rina Margolin and Mark Kuroczko for suggestions on editing the foreword.

Malcolm Margolin

Table of Contents

Foreword by Malcolm Margolin......................................9
Introduction by Frank F. Latta....................................19

Around the Horn to Yerba Buena...................................25
Crossing the San Joaquin Valley..................................31
Settling into the South Sierra Gold Country......................37
The Valley Indians and the Mountain Indians......................43
The Choinumne Language...49
Games..55
Indian Houses and Customs..59
Choinumne Cooking..63
Fishing and Hunting..71
Native Wild Life...75
Hunting Lore...79
Public Life and Education..87
Trip to Tulare Lake..93
Indian and Anglo Conflicts Begin................................101
Indian Morals...105
Crowded Out by Settlers...109
Return from Tulare Lake...111
Conflict and Tragedy..117

Index...124

Foreword

BY MALCOLM MARGOLIN

I n the spring of 1850, a former military officer born in Kentucky, William Mayfield, led his wife and three sons eastward over the Pacheco Pass toward the San Joaquin Valley and the gold fields beyond. As Thomas Jefferson Mayfield, then six years old, would recount much later, they were making their way through the tall, waving grass when "suddenly my daddy pointed over the tops of the bare hills ahead of us and exclaimed, 'Look there!' And there in the distance, until then lost to us in the haze, was our valley. A shining thread of light marked the Rio San Joaquin, flowing, as my mother said, 'through a crazy quilt of color.'

"How excited we all were. Everyone wanted to talk at once. Then someone noticed that what we had at first taken for clouds still further to the east was a high range of snow-covered peaks, their bases lost in the purple haze." Ecstatic with joy, the family descended into the luxuriant meadowlands where, wading through grasses as high as their stirrups, they stopped to bedeck themselves and their horses with wild flowers.

A tremendous awareness of beauty, itself like a "shining thread," runs through the narrative before us: of the grand beauty of the "primeval" San Joaquin Valley; of the splendid herds of elk and antelope that roamed freely over its seemingly limitless breadth; of flocks of cranes, geese, and ducks that darkened the sky with their numbers; of the great expanse of Tulare Lake, once the second largest lake west of the Mississippi; and especially of the Indian people whose long-established villages once rimmed the lakes and lined the rivers that flowed into the valley. It is a story of an extraordinary beauty, now much diminished, almost (but not entirely) lost to the modern world.

It is something of a miracle that the story itself was not also lost. That it survived at all is due to the collaboration between two singular men. One was Thomas Jefferson Mayfield, a white man who had grown up among the Choinumne Yokuts during the 1850s and who, with a few months to live, broke a self-imposed silence of more than sixty years to tell the story. The other was Frank F. Latta, a self-defined historian and ethnographer of the San Joaquin Valley, who convinced Mayfield to recount his memories and who then went on to arrange, edit, and eventually publish them at his own expense.

By a series of circumstances related in the chapters that follow, Mayfield, for a period of about ten years spanning childhood and adolescence, came to live among the Choinumne people of the Kings River area. He slept in their houses, joined them on their daily rounds, and followed them on their annual expeditions by tule boat to Tulare Lake. He spoke their language, wore their style of dress, ate their foods, absorbed many of their attitudes, and in short, lived for some ten years almost entirely like an Indian. His remarkable narrative represents, as far as I know, the only account of an outsider who ever lived among a California Indian people while they were still following their traditional ways.

Although the original narrative created by Mayfield and Latta covers the whole of Mayfield's life, only the first part dealing with his experiences among the Choinumne is reprinted in this edition. As the subsequent parts of the narrative explain, after he left the Choinumne in the early 1860s, Mayfield tried his hand at herding sheep and prospecting, making trips to Utah, Oregon, the high Sierra and the deserts of California in search of gold and other rare minerals. When not tramping the hills and deserts of the west with his burro, he would return to a small mining town in the southern San Joaquin Valley called Tailholt (later renamed White River), where he did odd jobs. Finally too old to prospect, he retired here to become something of a local legend, a grizzled old bachelor known to everyone as "Uncle Jeff."

Early settlers of the region often characterized the local Indians as thieves and murderers. Yet, paradoxically, life in the early mining communities of the San Joaquin Valley and the foothill region was, at least as Mayfield remembered it, one of overwhelming lawlessness and violence. In the latter part of the Mayfield narrative (not reprinted here) we find described in some detail robberies, gangs, rustling of livestock, rumors of buried treasure, and most noticeably, one murder after another—deaths involving not only strangers but members of Mayfield's own family.

It was into this harsh, Indian-hating, frontier world that Mayfield emerged after having spent most of his childhood among the Choinumne. Faced with hostility and prejudice whenever his association with the Indians was suspected, he fell silent about his childhood experiences. From the early 1860s until shortly before his death in 1928, he did not, as he said, spend as much as a total of one half hour talking to others about his life among the Choinumne. Ironically, this silence is undoubtedly what helped preserve the story. To have brought out his memories in an atmosphere of brutality and contempt would have surely altered them, perhaps giving them a defensive tone, perhaps eroding them until they became closer to what others wanted to hear. Instead, when at the very end of his life he found a receptive ear into which to pour his memories, they came bursting forth out of sixty years of protective silence with freshness, clarity of detail, and startling vivacity.

The person to whom Mayfield entrusted his memories was Frank F. Latta, a man many years his junior. Latta was born in 1892 in Stanislaus County, California. His mother was a teacher, his father a Presbyterian minister. When he was fourteen, a school teacher encouraged him to record the history of the school district by interviewing the original settlers of the area. From that early age almost until his death, Latta never stopped interviewing, ultimately collecting several thousand accounts from the Indians and pioneers of the San Joaquin Valley.

The early decades of the present century were an especially fertile time for historic and ethnographic research. The gold rush of 1849 was still a living memory, close to the hearts of the "old-timers" who hung around the grocery stores and gas stations of the small valley towns, eager to reminisce about how they had crossed the prairie in wagon trains, how they had staked out their first claims, how they had found (or more likely failed to find) gold, and how they eventually had moved into herding, farming, logging, or other rural occupations.

If the memories of the old-time settlers reached back to the gold rush era, the memories of many of the elderly Indians of the area went back much further. Still alive in the early decades of this century were many who remembered the traditional ways of life before they were disrupted—who remembered a world deeply rooted in the soil, rivers, and lakes of the San Joaquin Valley; a world that, having evolved and flourished for untold centuries, was now fading with a terrible and tragic rapidity.

The California Indian world was not one that an outsider could easily understand. At the time of the gold rush, an estimated 80,000 Indians were living in the San Joaquin Valley, a people generally referred to as Yokuts. While the Yokuts spoke a more or less common language, it was broken up into several quite distinct dialects. Nor were the Yokuts anything like a political or cultural unit. There was no Yokuts tribe, for example, but rather dozens of small nations, each with its territory, its leaders, and with customs and beliefs that were widely divergent. Adding to the complexity, yet other peoples lived in the foothills and mountains that rimmed the San Joaquin Valley, each of them speaking different languages and following different customs.

Latta threw himself into this rich complexity with the greatest of zeal. In a succession of vehicles, Latta—in later years often accompanied by his wife, Jean, and their four children—set out along dirt roads to the most remote corners of the San Joaquin Valley to record and photograph the Indian people. While supporting himself and his family mostly by teaching high school, he tirelessly did very basic, pioneering ethnographic research, sorting out the names and territories of the various Yokuts groups, using lists of words that he elicited from various native speakers to identify the dialects, collecting volumes of information on place names and on the customs and technological skills of the people he encountered. At reservations, Indian settlements, and in private homes throughout the Valley, Latta became a familiar sight, a tall, slender man nicknamed *Wee-chet-e*, man with "little sticks," so called because of the bundles of pencils he always carried with him for taking his voluminous notes.

It is clear from reading through the boxes of Latta's papers, now stored at the Yosemite National Park Research Library, that of the many thousands of interviews that Latta conducted among early pioneers and Indians, he valued the Mayfield material most highly. Indian people, of course, knew their own culture with much greater intimacy and detail than Mayfield could ever have known it. But Indians of that generation often did not speak English well—many, in fact, did not speak English at all—and being so immersed in their own culture they did not quite know how to interpret it for others: what to emphasize, what to describe. In Mayfield, Latta found a man who had not only lived within Indian culture, but who, as a member of the dominant society, had the perspective to sum it up and describe it in a way that corresponded with the thinking and categories of the Anglo mind.

Latta lost no time in publishing the Mayfield narratives as a series of newspaper articles. Then, within a year of Mayfield's death in 1928, a slender volume appeared published by the Tulare Times Press in an edition of five hundred. The book was titled *San Joaquin Primeval: Uncle Jeff's Story, A Tale of a San Joaquin Valley Pioneer and his Life with the Yokuts Indians*. It was a hastily done and unattractive hardcover book, fewer than one hundred pages in length, with the type jammed onto each page in double columns, badly printed, and without photos, maps, or other graphics. Latta himself was dissatisfied, and when donating a copy to the New York Public Library in 1931 he wrote: "Accept my apologies..., as we are disappointed in the booklet. It was printed from type used in a newspaper set-up and is quite crude in composition. Stanford University Press is now preparing to publish the same in a nice edition which will be upon the market as soon as business conditions warrant."

Stanford University Press had indeed expressed an interest in publishing another edition of *Uncle Jeff's Story*, and the Latta Archive at Yosemite National Park Research Library has a thick folder devoted to the correspondence between Latta and William Hawley Davis, editor. For a period of four years, while Davis kept trying to reach a decision about whether to publish the book, Latta continued to send him more and more Mayfield-related material. He sent additions, corrections, and amplifications to the original manuscript, apparently from his interview notes with

12

Mayfield. As he interviewed other Valley pioneers, he also sent in their comments whenever they corroborated something that Mayfield had said. He also began to collect photos: photos of Mayfield, of the places Mayfield mentioned, of life in the San Joaquin Valley.

For several years Latta kept sending new material, and Davis kept promising to reach a decision. When the decision finally came, however, it was negative. America was in the midst of an economic depression, money was scarce, and "Californiana" was not selling.

While the correspondence with Davis came to an end in 1934, the compiling of additions to the Mayfield book did not, and for years afterward Latta continued to assemble corrections, additions, corroborations, and photographs.

It was not until 1976 that Latta was finally able to republish the Mayfield narratives. Retitling the book *Tailholt Tales,* he brought it out under the imprint of Bear State Books, a publishing company that he and his family formed specifically to publish the results of their historic and ethnographic research.

Forty-seven years had elapsed between the publication of *Uncle Jeff's Story* and *Tailholt Tales*, nearly a half century of frustration coupled with steady accumulation of new material. While *Uncle Jeff's Story* was 88 pages long, *Tailholt Tales* came to 320 pages, largely due to these additions.

At the core of *Tailholt Tales* is the simple story that Mayfield had told years before, corrected and amplified, apparently from the original interview notes. This narrative is then interspersed with comments by Latta in his own voice, and further glossed with the inclusion of interviews with other early settlers who substantiated what Mayfield had said. The new edition also includes a foreword by the linguist and anthropologist John P. Harrington, a reminiscence by Latta about the life and personality of Harrington, notes on the history of Bear State Books and other Latta family projects, plus scores of photographs. Some of these photos are of Mayfield; some show places mentioned in the narrative, often much changed by the time the photos were taken; some are stills from a film that Latta helped produce, showing modern-day Yokuts dressed in animal skins and posed in reconstructed villages; some show Latta and his family pursuing their ethnographic research, vacationing in Mexico, and forming Bear State Books.

Tailholt Tales, in short, is not only *Uncle Jeff's Story* corrected and expanded, but a commentary on and concordance to *Uncle Jeff's Story* as well. The inclusion of family photos and tangential text were clearly intended to provide a full context for the Mayfield material—a multidimensional presentation of not only the Mayfield narrative but of the people who produced it. So many voices, however, along with the eclectic photos, give the second edition a scrapbook quality. Indicative of the changes between the two volumes is the fact that in *Uncle Jeff's Story*, Latta lists himself simply as editor—"Arranged by Frank F. Latta," to use his exact phrase. In *Tailholt Tales*, he lists himself as author, and with just cause. *Tailholt Tales* is largely a book of Latta's creation, in which the Mayfield narrative is a major but no longer exclusive part.

Anyone interested in the totality of San Joaquin Valley history, in its early pioneers, and in the life of its premier historian, Frank Latta, might do well to search out a copy of *Tailholt Tales* in a library or used book store. My own interests, however, lie with Mayfield's description of life among the Choinumne; and it is my hope that, cut back to the simplicity of the core story, this extraordinary narrative will reach a wider readership than the more thoroughly annotated version of 1976 might. Consequently, I have included only the material from the original *Uncle Jeff's Story*, adding from *Tailholt Tales* those amplifications and corrections that Latta presented as being in Mayfield's own voice, presumably from the original interview notes. I have also taken the liberty of rearranging the sequence of incidents to form a more coherent narrative.

The account before us is clearly one of the most remarkable and valuable documents in the entire range of California Indian material. As John P. Harrington wrote in his foreword to *Tailholt Tales*: "Few readers will realize that this information which Mr. Latta has preserved lies on the very outskirts of human knowledge and that he has rescued practically all of these facts from oblivion." Indeed, the work before us has not only major ethnographic facts about how people hunted, fished, cooked, and built their houses, but insights into the manners of everyday life—intimate glimpses into how people washed their hands and faces, for example, or how they salted their fresh greens.

More than a compendium of valuable facts, the Mayfield narrative also manages to catch something of a flavor, a tone, a way of being, that is generally absent from more conventional anthropological works. In places we can almost hear the voices of the old people staying awake most of a cold winter night to keep the house fires going, of dozens of young boys playing Indian football, of mothers teaching their children to swim, of men excitedly commenting upon an immense flock of geese rising up from Tulare Lake.

For those who are hungry to know more about the old ways of life in California, the Mayfield narrative offers tremendous riches; and in the face of such a gift, it seems petty to criticize. It would be as if a starving person, after having been given an immense banquet, were to complain that a few of the dishes were not cooked to perfection. Yet it should be acknowledged that for all its undeniable virtues, the narrative before us does have some important shortcomings.

To begin, we must recognize that these reminiscences were dictated some 65 years ago by a man with almost no schooling who had spent much of his adult life prospecting for gold and doing odd jobs around the small towns of the San Joaquin Valley. Despite his extraordinary childhood experiences, he was in many ways a man of his times, and these were hardly the most sensitive of times. The modern reader cannot help but wince at certain of Mayfield's attitudes and expressions. In particular, his referring to Indian women as "mokees" or "squaws," likely done with affection, is jarring to the modern ear and insulting to native people today. The editor of this volume therefore took it upon himself to change such expressions to "woman" or "women."

Other biases were, however, more embedded in the text, and these were not altered. Most troublesome are the disparaging references to the Monache. Now generally called the "Mono," "Western Mono," or "Sierra Mono," these people were in the 1850s relative newcomers to the area, having slowly migrated across the Sierra from the Mono Lake and Great Basin areas into the more hospitable lands long used by Yokuts groups. The Yokuts viewed these people with considerable alarm and hostility, and this is how Mayfield presents them—as murderous, thieving, untrustworthy people. Yet anyone who is acquainted with Mono traditional life or who knows personally members of today's Mono community will surely recognize that such sentiments reflect the biases of the Yokuts and the fears of the white settlers more than any truth about the Mono people.

It is also necessary to remember that Mayfield was a six-year-old boy when he first took up residence with the Choinumne, and still a teenager when their traditional way of life came to an end. His experiences and his memories reflect all the enthusiasms and limitations of his age and gender. Thus we find wondrously detailed descriptions of how to play field games, how to build pigeon traps, and how to construct a fish gig, while other important aspects of Yokuts culture—religious philosophy, the gathering of basketry material, the making of baskets, girls' coming of age ceremonies, etc.—are almost entirely absent from this narrative.

Finally, there is the inescapable fact that Mayfield was not an Indian. As the last chapters of this book poignantly demonstrate, he was, in the end, very much a white man, clearly and perhaps tragically a product of his time.

In short, the volume before us is not a full and well-balanced depiction of Choinumne life. Rather, it is an eyewitness account by a particular person who lived among the Choinumne at a particular time, and who told the story of that time with verve, passion, and (despite his limitations) great fidelity. The story that he told, while less than perfect, is nonetheless amazing, providing us with a unique description of the Choinumne world, a world into which it is hoped the reader will move with a sense of awe and wonderment, and perhaps with appreciation for Latta and Mayfield, the two unusual men who worked so hard to keep the memory of that world alive.

Indian Summer portrays a world which is now tragically faded. The herds of pronghorn antelope, the flocks of geese, the grand stretches of oak forest, and the luxuriant, flowery meadows have all been dreadfully reduced. Even Tulare Lake, once measuring hundreds of square miles, has been rendered insignificant. As an elderly Yokuts woman named Yoimut, born on the shores of Tulare Lake, complained some seventy years ago, where there had once been natural beauty there was now only "cotton, cotton, cotton."

Likewise, the Choinumne people and their culture have been severely reduced. They have been driven from their lands, while their customs and beliefs have been mocked and sometimes even outlawed for most of the last hundred and fifty years. In the face of such assault, many Choinumne people have lost most of their traditional ways. Others have found that they can continue to be Indian only on the fringes of the dominant society, as if being Indian were a crime, something that can be done only in secret.

Yet, while greatly diminished, neither the beauty of the land nor the greatness of its native people has been entirely destroyed. In the remnants of an oak forest, in the honking of geese settling into a patch of wetland, in the soaring of a hawk, or in the fragrance of a spring breeze, one can now and then still catch a glimpse of the ancient grandeur.

So too with the people. The open-hearted hospitality and generosity with which the Indian people greeted the first white settlers—carrying their goods (and often their persons) across rivers and supplying them with food from their own surplus—is, despite everything that has happened, still very much a part of Indian culture today. The Choinumne dialect, cherished by Mayfield as he recalled the vocabulary of his childhood, is still a living language, spoken by a handful of elders. Likewise, many of the old customs, attitudes, and beliefs described by Mayfield can even yet be found among the Choinumne and other Yokuts people today.

Like the natural beauty of the area, Indian life has been pushed to the edge. Forced to struggle and adapt, admittedly fragile and threatened, it nevertheless, miraculously, continues to exist.

Today, at least at more optimistic moments, one feels that there is a new attitude developing among many people. The old frontier mentality that gave the dominant culture the unquestionable right to exploit other people and abuse the land seems on the wane. Environmental groups have arisen in recent years and are struggling to keep the land from further degradation, and perhaps even restore some of it to a state of greater natural beauty. Likewise there are those within the Indian community who, even at this late date, are working hard to assure the continuation of their cultures and restoration of Indian rights. Native languages are being studied by a younger generation, elders are being listened to with respect, songs are being relearned, rituals long dormant are again being performed, and Indian children are being taught pride rather than shame in their heritage. It is in hopeful times such as these that we offer this exceptional narrative. May the vision of a magnificent past inspire and nourish those who are working toward a better future.

Introduction

BY FRANK F. LATTA

U ncle Jeff's Story," which is to follow this introduction, is almost the dying word of one of the most interesting characters the San Joaquin Valley produced.

Sometime in May of 1928 the writer was collecting information from an Indian in the hills east of Visalia. At the end of more than four hours of work it was found that the information was of practically no value because of the misunderstanding of an Indian word at the beginning of the interview. Greatly disappointed and discouraged, the writer drove to Visalia and called on Mrs. John Cutler. In the historical work done by the writer, Mrs. Cutler, with her happy philosophy and deep appreciation, has proven a constant aid and encouragement.

Relating the experience to Mrs. Cutler, the wish was expressed that some white person could be found who had been raised by, or who had lived with the Indians. A person who had lived with the Indians could interpret all words, and the meaning could be recorded quickly and accurately. Otherwise the person collecting the data had to understand almost as much of the Indian dialect as the Indian himself in order to arrive correctly at the meaning of one word. Of course, this was asking too much, more than was possible; but, as it was expressed at the time, "it cost nothing to wish for plenty."

After the wish was expressed Mrs. Cutler raised her hand and said that if the writer would start out and look for such a person and not give up, sooner or later he would find what he was looking for. At this we both laughed, and the writer arose to come to Tulare.

Driving directly to Tulare, and parking the car in front of Tripletts' Store, the writer stepped to the curb just in time to meet Mr. M.C. Zumwalt. Zumwalt said, "I was just now going to the store to telephone to you; Mike Mitchell of Ducor knows an old man at White River who was raised by the Indians on Kings River. He has been over this part of the valley with them, and on Tulare Lake, and he knows more Indian than all the Indians in the country." Just like Zumwalt, wasn't it? Nothing had been said to him about what was wanted, but there he was with the very thing that was needed.

Surely, this was too good to be true. Several previous reports of other cases of a like nature had been investigated, only to prove disappointing. However, noon of the next day saw the writer in Ducor where a short discussion with Mike Mitchell served to more than support the account given by Zumwalt.

With Mitchell as guide, the drive to White River was soon made. There, seated on the edge of the porch in front of the store, sat the object of my search. After less than five minutes of questioning I knew that Thomas Jefferson Mayfield, or Uncle Jeff, as everyone about White River called him, had a great deal more information than I had even dared to hope for.

For ten years, from the time he was eight until he was about eighteen, he had lived with the San Joaquin Valley Indians on Kings River. On their large tule rafts he had traveled with them to Tulare Lake on their fishing expeditions. He had hunted with them, fished with them, and shot with them with their own weapons. Then, too, his whole life was just as interesting. He had stories of the first bandits of the San Joaquin, prospecting in Death Valley when it really was the valley of death, the Mojave Desert in the seventies, murder and mystery stories of the old valley settlements, and many other things of a like nature.

It all seemed too good to be true.

But Uncle Jeff was well past eighty years of age, and, in addition, he was then suffering from an attack of influenza.

Mitchell and the writer were both very much concerned at his sickness, and decided that his story had better be recorded as fast as possible. Only enough time was taken that first day to learn what to expect in the nature of information, and an immediate return to Tulare was made.

The remainder of that afternoon and most of the next night was spent in typewriting questions for him to answer; a vocabulary such as was probably used by the Indians, questions about their life, marriage, initiation ceremonies, hunting, fishing, weapons, dress, games, music, cooking, houses, and a thousand other things.

In the morning the writer returned to White River, arriving there at about ten a.m. An immediate start was made. The list of questions was gone over and the answers to them quickly recorded. Without as much as ten minutes of lost time or a stop for lunch, this was continued until after six p.m., eight hours or more, and at that time Uncle Jeff was as fresh and as interested as he had been at the beginning.

The writer was with him every weekend until the middle of June, and every day for two weeks afterward. Then, through the summer, many more weekends were spent at White River, and another week of full time, making in all more than six weeks of time, working on an average of more than eight hours a day.

In this time his story was almost completed and recorded as nearly in his exact words as possible. His expression was good; his understanding of what was wanted complete. He had an absolutely accurate memory and the mind of a scientist. When a question was asked about Indian life he was ready with a comprehensive answer. Those things he had studied over for more than seventy-five years. No one with whom he came in contact had any understanding, or appreciation, of what he knew, and he had never discussed his life with the Indians.

Mr. Bellah, who conducted the store at White River and has been there continuously for more than twenty years, had seen Uncle Jeff almost daily during that time. He told the writer that Uncle Jeff had talked more for Mike Mitchell in thirty minutes than he had heard him talk in twenty years.

It was interesting to observe the change that came over the man as the work progressed. At first he was reluctant to discuss his life with the Indians. But as he found that someone else was as much interested as he was, and was willing to preserve what information he had without any changing or ridicule, he became as enthusiastic as a boy.

But we must let Uncle Jeff tell his own story, the beginning of which was gained last. He had suffered a stroke of paralysis while he was alone in his little cabin at White River and had been removed to the county hospital in Visalia. This was in September of 1928. He was not feeling well and was seated on the edge of his bed trying to make his story complete by giving the writer an account of his family, their trip to Yerba Buena, their passage through Pueblo de San Jose, over the Pacheco Pass, and then across the San Joaquin Valley to Las Mariposas. It could be easily seen that he could go no farther that day and the writer bade him good-bye. Although the writer did not know it for several weeks, as he was descending the steps in front of the hospital Uncle Jeff collapsed in the arms of the nurse, dead.

This is Uncle Jeff's own story. The writer has tried not to profane it in changing the form of expression. The events, not obtained in order, have been placed so as to make a connected story. The veracity of Uncle Jeff is attested by an unlimited number of persons who have known him for sixty years or more. John Guthrie, of White River, said, "Uncle Jeff has never told a lie to anyone. You can accept any statement he makes as absolute truth." The accuracy of the story as far as it can be checked is one hundred percent.

Remember—Uncle Jeff attended school less than six weeks. He had never studied history. He only knew of the War of 1812 as he had heard his father mention it. He felt embarrassed at his lack of knowledge of the events with which his story begins, and did not know just how much of it was accurate.

His daddy was a real man. He helped Captain Tivy make the first survey of Tulare county. He placed the first hogs on Tulare Lake. He had run horses and cattle over the greater part of the San Joaquin Valley. He had captured wild horses on the west side, fought Monache Indians on the east side and was known far and wide in the San Joaquin during the fifties and early sixties.

"My daddy" to Uncle Jeff was almost a tradition. After he was eight years old he had known him only a few months when he was killed during the Indian war of 1862, in what is now Inyo county, when captain of a troop of Visalia Dragoons. He always spoke of his father as "my daddy."

F.F. LATTA
April 8, 1929
Tulare, California

Indian Summer

Around the Horn to Yerba Buena

MY DADDY was born in Kentucky. His folks had a large plantation and a great many slaves and race horses. They were quite wealthy and my daddy traveled a great deal when he was young.

When my daddy was about eighteen a man by the name of [Andrew] Jackson was having some trouble with a lot of Englishmen. He needed help, and so my daddy went with him to a place called New Orleans. There, in the swamps, they had a battle with the Englishmen and ran them out into the water. My daddy always said that this man Jackson was a real fighter, and Jackson liked my daddy, too, because he made him a lieutenant.

While my daddy was with Jackson, he met some men who had been to a place away out west, and they told him so many stories about this place that after a few years he went out there. There he met a man named [Sam] Houston. This man Houston was having trouble with some Mexicans. My daddy went with him and they drove those Mexicans clear out of the country, and Houston made my daddy a captain, and he made himself president of a country he called Texas.

In Brazos County, Texas, my daddy met and married a Miss Maria Curd. There were three children born to them; John Mayfield, about 1826; Ben Mayfield, about 1831; and Thomas Jefferson Mayfield, myself, about 1843.

After my daddy was with Houston he thought he would quit fighting and settle down, but this man Houston turned his country over to Uncle Sam, and those same Mexicans came back again and did a lot of mean things. So Uncle Sam started in to give them another whipping. Then my daddy went with a man called [Alexander W.] Doniphan down through a place called Chihuahua toward Mexico City. They gave those Mexicans a pretty good whipping. This man Doniphan liked my daddy so well that he wrote a letter to Uncle Sam, and Uncle Sam made my daddy a colonel.

When Uncle Sam was through with the Mexicans, and didn't need my daddy in Texas any more, he told my daddy that he had taken a place called California away from those Mexicans and that he wanted a lot of Americans to go out there and live so that those Mexicans wouldn't do any more mean things like they had in Texas. He also said that if my daddy would go, he would take him and his family out to California with one of his army wagon trains.

So my daddy got ready, and they started to California along a road they called the Santa Fe Trail. After they had gone a long way they received news that some Indians called Mescalero Apaches were on the warpath and had massacred some of the people with a wagon train ahead of us.

Then Uncle Sam's officers held a pow-wow and decided that no women or children could go with the train. Of course my daddy couldn't go on and leave us, so those officers told him to go back to Galveston, and they would take him to a place called Yerba Buena [San Francisco] on one of Uncle Sam's transports.

Of the trip from Galveston to Yerba Buena I remember very little that I am sure was not gained from the discussion of older members of the family. We were six months and a few days on the water. Practically every day of this time was spent in the midst of a raging storm. We were blown around Cape Horn completely out of control and expected to go on the rocks at any moment. However, we were blown around the rocks and into clear water on the Pacific side. During this rounding of the horn there were only three men able to go on deck and they were helpless in the storm.

On the trip up the Pacific conditions were as bad. We were blown hundreds of miles out to sea, out of our course, and were four weeks in getting back on our course. When we arrived in Yerba Buena there were only three able-bodied men to bring the ship into port and to anchor.

Of this trip I distinctly remember being cooped up between decks for what seemed to me years, and also occasional glimpses of mountainous seas. I also remember my mother holding me close to her together with my older brother, Ben, when we were in particularly dangerous places.

There are only one or two things about the landing at Yerba Buena that I remember clearly. We anchored among a sea of idle ships and at what seems yet to have been a great distance from shore. Our small boat, which carried the passengers ashore, landed to the left, or south, of a considerable marsh. There was a small wooden wharf where our boat landed, and a large slimy mud flat. I remember seeing stoves that had apparently been dumped off in the mud.

Of Yerba Buena I remember very little. We were all in a hurry to get to the mines. As I recollect, there were several adobe buildings and a cluster of tents and wooden frames with canvas or some sort of white cloth tacked over them. The place was hilly and covered with brush and scrub oak. It was not a large place and the buildings I have mentioned were built on the hills in the brush without any attempt at street grading. Near the water the roadways were seas of mud.

We spent only a few days in Yerba Buena. My daddy had read [John C.] Fremont's book *[Report of the Exploring Expedition to the Rocky Mountains in the Year 1842, and to Oregon and North California in the Years 1843-44]*, and he was going to the Fremont mines at Las Mariposas. So he bought three pack animals and four saddle horses with equipment and we started out. Leaving Yerba Buena we traveled south toward Pueblo de San Jose. The first night we camped at a small stream west of

27

the Mission de San Jose [Mission Santa Clara?] but did not see the mission buildings.

I remember that a number of the long-horned cattle so familiar to us in Texas came along. Just before dark an Indian vaquero rode by and drove the cattle toward the east. This vaquero was a very interesting person and rode a fine horse. He was quite dark and straight and rode as though he was a part of the horse. He had what we used to call a mochila saddle. The wooden tree was separate from the leather covering, or mochila. When the horse was saddled the tree was first cinched in place and then the mochila was thrown over it. At night the mochila formed a good mattress and protection against the dampness of the earth. When a horse bucked off its rider the mochila generally went flying through the air after him.

The Indian dismounted and talked to my daddy in Spanish. He said that he was riding for a Spaniard who lived nearby. We all crowded close to look at his silver-mounted bridle and spurs, and we watched him drive the cattle away.

The next day about noon we arrived at Pueblo de San Jose. We stopped long enough to lay in our last supplies, as my daddy did not expect to be able to buy anything more until we reached Las Mariposas.

In my memory I have only a picture of San Jose as a quiet, sleepy village. The row of adobe buildings where we stopped formed one side of a large open square. I did not want to dismount as there were a number of large, hungry-looking dogs growling and sniffing about, and there were a number of renegade-looking Mexicans sitting on a bench against the wall in front of the store where we were stopped. The Mexicans tried not to let us see them looking at us. They would keep their faces turned away, or they would look down at the ground. Several times I caught them looking at us, but they would quickly turn their heads away as soon as I looked in their direction. I remember that my daddy called them greasers, and said that they would be a hard lot to meet after dark.

The second night we spent at John Gilroy's ranch. I do not remember that we saw him, although we camped near the ranch buildings. During the night we were bothered by cattle. They made quite a fuss and we were watchful for fear they would run over us. We drove them away several times, but in the morning they were standing a short distance away in a circle about our camp.

Leaving Gilroy's ranch early in the morning, we followed a trail that led away to the southeast. This trail was to lead us to Pacheco Pass, which was the best route into the San Joaquin Valley south of Livermore's Pass. The way was through very low foothills to a broad, gravelly creek bottom covered with sycamores. We followed this creek to a high, round peak, or bluff, which stood close to the south bank. There we camped for the night close to the creek, which was a fresh, clear stream about thirty feet wide and a foot or more in depth.

While we were making camp a party of native Californians came from upstream and stopped for a few minutes. They talked Spanish to my daddy and told him that we were camped on El Arroyo de Pacheco and that El Paso de Pacheco lay ahead of us. They also told him that El Arroyo de San Luis Gonzaga headed with El Arroyo de Pacheco and that their party came from El Rancho de San Luis, east of the pass. They assured us that it was an easy day's travel to El Rancho de San Luis and that just a few miles beyond was the Valle de San Joaquin and El Rio de San Joaquin flowing northward down the middle of the valley. My daddy was so well-pleased with their appearance and freedom in giving us information that he decided to stop at El Rancho de San Luis the next night. It was long before sunup when we started up the creek toward the pass.

Crossing the San Joaquin Valley

F OUR WHOLE TRIP from Texas to Kings River I remember the Pacheco Pass portion the best. In fact, my first real clear recollection begins as we were ascending the western slope leading toward the pass. We were all so anxious for our first glimpse of the Valle de San Joaquin, as our Californian acquaintances had called it, that I am sure we all remembered the Pacheco Pass and the first view it gave us at the summit.

After we had almost reached the summit, I begged to be allowed to ride on one of the pack animals. I had been riding on a folded blanket behind my mother's saddle, and from there could not see ahead. She did not like to have me ride the pack animals, as they were loose and might brush me off when they passed under low branches. But as the country grew more level and we came to a large, flat meadow, she had my oldest brother place me on top of one of the packs.

I remember that there were five or six deer feeding in the meadow, and that they did not run away, but watched us closely as we passed at a distance of about two hundred yards.

As we left the meadow and again entered the timber to the east, I remember the scene so well. My daddy and brother, Ben, were riding ahead. Then came the three pack animals, mine being the third. Brother John came behind me driving the loose animals. Then came mother, the last of the procession, interested in the new valley we were about to enter, but watching me most of the time. I remember that I proudly smiled back at her from my perch on the pack ahead, and that she returned my smile. I can see her yet. This is the last real picture that I have of my mother, as she died within a year.

Within a few minutes after we entered the timber we came to

the eastern slope, and through an opening in the trees we could see a large canyon through which my daddy concluded ran El Arroyo de San Luis Gonzaga.

We followed down a long ridge to our right on the south side of the canyon. Here, for the first time, we noticed that a passage had been made with wagons just a short time previous to our coming. Brush had been cleared away, and a few trees had been felled and dragged to one side. The leaves on the felled trees were still partly green. We followed the wagon trail down the ridge.

So far we were all disappointed because we could not see the valley, and we were growing more restless and anxious all the time. There were always trees and brush in the way and there seemed to be a high range of bare hills fifteen or twenty miles further on. In addition, the view ahead was obscured by a purplish haze. Finally we rode out on a bare point, and halted in order to rest the animals and to talk. We could see that there was a fairly extensive, bowl-shaped valley between us and the bare hills to the east. There was a strong west wind blowing, and it was waving the tall grasses in the valley and changing its floor into shifting splotches of a green and yellowish green.

Suddenly my daddy pointed over the tops of the bare hills ahead of us and exclaimed, "Look there!" And there in the distance, until then lost to us in the haze, was our valley. A shining thread of light marked El Rio de San Joaquin flowing, as my mother said, "through a crazy quilt of color."

How excited we all were. Everyone wanted to talk at once. Then someone noticed, still farther to the east, that what we had at first taken for clouds was a high range of snow-covered peaks, their bases lost in the purple haze.

Finally we started on and passed down the long ridge, which my daddy called a "hog's back," to the small valley below. There we found the grass we had seen from above to be wild oats. They stood as high as our stirrups and were as thick as they could grow. My daddy said that was the finest country he had ever seen.

We followed along El Arroyo de San Luis to where it passed through a narrow opening in the bare hills to the San Joaquin plains below. There, under a grove of large cottonwoods and sycamores, we found the buildings of El Rancho de San Luis.

Of the ranch buildings I remember only a long, low adobe with loopholed walls. Here we were made welcome by a pretty native Californian, who talked Spanish to us and took my mother and me inside with her.

The inside of the building was of interest to me as I had not been in one just like it before. There was an earthen floor which had been smoothed and beaten hard. In one corner was a raised adobe platform about the size of a modern blacksmith's forge. There the cooking was done. In the opposite corner was a crude bed made of a cowhide stretched over a rough wooden frame. There were two chairs in the room, and a few garments hanging on the wall.

After a short visit we made camp under a large cottonwood tree on the bank of the creek a few yards northeast of the building. Here there was a large deep pool of water. I have always remembered that place as one of the most ideal I have ever seen. The tall, green grass, the cool, clear water, and the trees with their fresh leaves made as pretty a spot as one could wish.

We left Rancho de San Luis early the next morning before anyone was stirring at the adobe house, and passed down the creek about three miles. By this time we were out on the level plains, and the creek was a wide shallow bed of gravel with a small stream of water wandering about it.

Leaving the stream, we started across the plains in an easterly direction. We had been told at El Rancho de San Luis that we would in this way arrive at El Rio de San Joaquin where there was a ford. By this time we could see what had caused the mass of color so noticeable from the mountain the day before. The entire plain, as far as we could see, was covered with wild flowers. Almost all of the flowers were new to us.

Along the creek were many blue lupines, some of them growing on bushes six and eight feet high. The low foothills were covered with two pretty, lily-like flowers, one tall and straight-stemmed with a cluster of lavender, bell-shaped flowers at the top and the other a purple, ball-shaped blossom on a similar stem.

As we passed below the hills the whole plain was covered with great patches of rose, yellow, scarlet, orange and blue. The colors did not seem to mix to any great extent. Each kind of flower liked a certain kind of soil best and some of the patches of one color were a mile or more across.

I believe that we were more excited out there on the plains among the wild flowers than we had been when we saw the valley for the first time from the mountain the day before. Several times we stopped to pick the different kinds of flowers and soon we had our horses and packs decorated with masses of all colors.

My daddy had traveled a great deal and it was not easy to get him excited about wild flowers, or pretty scenery. But he said that he would not have believed that such a place existed if he had not seen it himself. And my mother cried with joy, and wanted to make a home right here in the midst of it all.

For my own part, I have never seen anything to equal the virgin San Joaquin Valley before there was a plow or a fence within it. I have always loved nature and have liked to live close to her. Many times when traveling alone and night has overtaken me, I have tied my horse and rolled up in my saddle blanket and slept under a bank, or among the wild flowers, or on the desert under a bush. I remember those experiences as the greatest in my life. The two most beautiful remembrances I have are the virgin San Joaquin and my mother.

Many times since have I seen all of the things I saw on that first trip through the valley. But they were all new then, and strange, and they made an impression that has not faded in the 78 years that have since passed. I do not mean by this that I have ever been back to El Paso de Pacheco, or to San Jose, or to San Francisco, for

I have never been over that trail since that spring day in 1850. When I think of those things, I see them as I saw them from my perch on the pack horse.

There were great dens of squirrels. They had thrown the soil up in many places to a height of two feet or more over an area of thirty yards square. Over this area their burrows were thick, and they would stand and bark at us by the hundreds as we approached. When we came close they would disappear, but as soon as we had passed they would stand braver than ever and bark at us as long as we were in hearing. Farming has destroyed most of their dens, and they have almost all been killed off where they were thickest in those days.

In some places badgers had either thrown the earth up much as the squirrels had, or they had driven out the squirrels and enlarged and appropriated their burrows.

I also remember glimpses of great droves of antelope standing out against the horizon at a distance, but we did not see any of them at close range. We also saw, to our right, a band of rapidly moving animals. My daddy said that these were horses. They kept at a distance, but seemed to be watching and following us.

When we neared the San Joaquin River we saw about twenty elk. We had approached quite close to them, but had not seen them at once, and they were hurrying away through a low swale, or dry slough, which paralleled the river. I will always remember how quickly they disappeared and how clever they were at making use of the cover. There were a few oak trees near, and they kept these between us and themselves. They lowered their heads with their horns against their necks and shoulders and sneaked along as rapidly as a horse could run.

We also saw some tracks along the river that my daddy said were made by bear. They must have been grizzlies, as I have found since that they were the only bear along the San Joaquin.

The most amusing sight I remember on the plains before we reached the San Joaquin River was a large flock of sandhill cranes.

We passed within forty yards of some of them and they hardly noticed us. Quite a large group of them were holding a sort of pow-wow. They would all jabber a while and then they would do a sort of fandango. We laughed at them for a long while, they were so sober and earnest about it.

We had been told at the San Luis Ranch that there was a ferry about 25 miles north, where the Merced River emptied into the San Joaquin. They said that this ferry had only been established a few months. But we had decided that a trip to the ferry would take us too far out of our way, and intended to use the ford they had described.

As we approached the river we found the water quite high, and had some difficulty in reaching the river. We finally reached the bank over some high ground. The river was too high to ford. So my daddy unloaded the pack animals and made them swim across. Then my mother and brothers swam their horses across, taking my daddy's horse with them. He had tied all of our ropes together and they took one end of this long line across with them. Then my daddy made a raft of dead willow branches, and ferried our supplies across. He accomplished this by tying one end of the long line to the raft. John tied the other end to a tree on the east bank. Then he mounted the raft and poled it away from the bank. As it drifted downstream the rope pulled it around to the east bank over a circular course.

On the east side of the river we experienced a great deal more trouble than we had on the west. It took us several hours to find our way around and through the sloughs that extended many miles east of the San Joaquin River.

The things I remembered best about this portion of our trip across the San Joaquin Valley were the great clouds of blackbirds that arose as we passed and the great growth of tules. Those tules must have been twenty feet high and two or more inches in thickness. We were as completely lost in them as we would have been in a forest.

Settling into the
South Sierra Gold Country

A FTER SEVERAL DAYS of plunging through tules and mud, and swimming and fording sloughs, we came out on a rolling, sandy slope country. Traveling eastward across this plain through the same wild flowers we had seen to the west, we finally encountered a trail, or what was really a wandering wagon road. Upon meeting several horsemen who were traveling along this road we found that it led to the Fremont Mines, as Las Mariposas was then called by the Americans. We traveled to our destination with the horsemen we had met.

My daddy was disappointed in the Fremont Mines. He had always been in an unsettled country and at the mines he found a great crowd of miners racing around, buying and selling claims and doing some mining. Everything for miles around was staked. So he decided to move farther south. I do not believe that we were there more than four or five weeks.

At this time, as I recollect, there had been no rush south of Las Mariposas, and we started south to the San Joaquin River where it flows westward from the Sierra. It was my daddy's plan to prospect that river for gold. We packed up again and started out in the same order that we had made the trip from Yerba Buena to Las Mariposas.

We arrived at the San Joaquin opposite an Indian rancheria. Here the river bank was quite high, and the water about one hundred yards across. I believe that this place was later called Cassidy's Ford. At any rate it was near where that ford was later.

A large group of Indians, numbering probably forty, were bathing in the south edge of the stream. As I remember, the group was composed mostly of young people. They all appeared very much excited at seeing our party, but did not seem afraid of us.

We sat on our horses a while and watched the bathers. Some of them were washing their hair. They would lean over, allowing their long hair to fall forward into the water. Then they would comb it with their fingers.

They soon became too deeply interested in us to go on with their bathing, and several of them swam to our side of the river. By this time we had dismounted, and were trying to decide whether to attempt a crossing there, or to follow the north bank of the river toward the hills.

My daddy found that one of the Indians could understand a little Spanish and this Indian encouraged him to cross the river, saying that his people would help him. So they made preparations to again ferry the river, as we had done before when crossing the valley from the San Luis Ranch to Las Mariposas.

While the animals were being unpacked I stayed near my mother, and she kept close watch over me, as eight or ten of the Indians, many of them wearing no clothing at all, were crowding about looking at me, excitedly talking to one another.

Finally a young girl about sixteen years of age offered to take me on her back and swim the river with me. At this my mother took me in her arms and held me close to her, motioning for the Indians to go away. She called to my daddy, and he ran to us, thinking that some hostile move had been made. He had fought the Mescalero Apaches for years, and knew Indians well. He soon saw that the Indians were all right and told my mother to let the girl carry me across, as I would be safer with her than I would on one of our horses.

So my mother took off my clothes and put me on the back of the Indian girl. I clasped my hands around her neck, and she took my feet under her arms and waded into the water.

Soon she started swimming with a long, overhand stroke. She was as slippery as could be, and I was afraid of being carried away by the current and clung to her neck so close that she could not breathe. Several times she stopped swimming and reached up and pulled my arms down until she recovered her breath. Then she started on again after each stop, until we arrived at the south edge of the stream in shallow water. She stood me in the water, which was about a foot deep, near a sandbar. During this time all of the Indian women and children from the rancheria had accumulated where we were about to land, and they crowded around me and laughed and talked to each other about me and called me *"chólo wé-chep"* (little white boy). I did not know their language then, but I have always felt sure that they were also telling each other how cute I was.

The girl who had carried me across the river was very proud of me and, holding to my hand, kept the rest of the Indians at a distance of several feet. She would talk to me and laugh, but of course I understood nothing she said, and re- membered only the words I mentioned before.

After we had crossed the river we spent several hours at the rancheria. Then we packed our animals again and traveled several miles upstream before we made camp. During the en- tire distance we were accompanied by a large group of Indians from the rancheria. After dark they left, but were back in the morning before sunrise with acorn bread and fresh meat for us.

Once I read some of Fremont's writing about his experi- ences with the Indians and he mentioned them as always expecting presents. I have had the Indians keep me for years and I know they expected no pay in return, and I feel sure that when those Indians brought us the meat and acorn bread that they did not expect anything in return.

The next day, after leaving the Indians, we proceeded up the river to where Fort Miller was soon built. There we found a couple of white men building a ferry. My daddy decided to stay there for a while and prospect the sand in the river. He soon found that there was some gold in it and built a long flume and sluice box of split logs in which to wash the sand.

During this time we were camped on a sandbar above the level of the water in the river. About the time my daddy had his sluice box done we had several days of real hot weather. It must have been about the first of July. There had been some discussion about high water, but we were not alarmed. I believe that the Indians had told us that there would be a flood. However, we had made no preparations to move, as we had felt that we were perfectly safe where we were.

There were several things that happened about this time that I remember quite distinctly. The Indians still kept in touch with us, and brought us meat and bread. This we used almost entirely, as we did not have a large supply of our own, and it was a long trip to Stockton for more. They also made me a present of a fine bow and a half dozen arrows.

One afternoon, while playing on the ferryboat with an Indian about my own age I slipped and fell in the water. I could not swim and of course immediately went under. When I came up the Indian boy was lying on his stomach with the upper part of his body hanging over the edge of the boat. I would surely have drowned if it had not been for him. He was not as big as I was, but he could swim like a fish. He grabbed me by the hair and towed me around the edge of the boat to shallow water where I could wade to shore. It was a narrow escape, and I never forgot that Indian boy. I knew him for many years afterward. His name was Koo-nance and he belonged to the tribe [Dumna] that had a rancheria near where Millerton was later located.

One afternoon I had been shooting at a mark on the sand-bar below our camp with my bow and arrows. I left them out there overnight. During the night we were awakened and found several inches of water within our tent. The river was rising rapidly and we rushed about in the dark, working hard to save our supplies and equipment. The thing that worried me most was my bow and arrows. I waded around in the water looking for them but was unable to find them, as they had been carried away before our tent was flooded. While I was looking for them the folks missed me and began a search for me. I soon appeared and they were glad to see me, but made me stay with our pile of equipment high up on the river bank.

The next morning we were a discouraged family. We had lost part of our supplies, and the flume and sluice box were entirely gone. No one had known anything about conditions on the river except the Indians, and no one had paid any attention to what they said. At least, we had not expected any such rise of water as came.

We camped on the bank of the river for several days. The water rose high above where we had been camped on the sandbar. During this time we learned from the Indians that the river would be much as it was then until late in the summer. By this time about twenty Americans had gathered about the ferry and were prospecting the surrounding country.

After much discussion my daddy decided that he would move further south and make a permanent settlement on Kings River. He had been over there a few weeks previous to our being flooded out and liked the country on Kings River very much. Mining did not appeal to him and he concluded he had enough of it.

So we packed up and traveled south again until we arrived at the north bank of Kings River at a point about where Centerville was later built. My daddy wanted to locate either in the mountains or in the foothills near the valley. He wanted to raise horses and cattle. Finally he decided that a foothill location would place him close to the free valley feed during the spring, and also the later mountain feed during the summer. I believe that this was the same reason that many of the first settlers in the valley selected foothill locations. In many localities the valley plains furnished free range until the late seventies.

We followed up the north bank of Kings River to the first good-sized stream flowing into it from the north. There, on the point of land formed by Kings River on the south and Sycamore Creek on the east, we again made camp.

There were many fine oak trees near. Sycamore Creek contained plenty of water and fish, and we felt sure that it would have running water in it all summer. If the water in Sycamore Creek should fail, then we would have Kings River nearby.

My Daddy and my older brothers, John and Ben, felled a tall oak tree and split it into shakes. From these shakes they built a two-room shanty. The roof and sides were entirely of shakes. They also built a large stone fireplace. Almost in front of the house, and only a few yards distant, stood an immense oak tree.

The Valley Indians
and the Mountain Indians

WHEN WE FIRST came to Kings River we met quite a number of Indians. They were of the same open-hearted, friendly disposition as those we had met on the San Joaquin. I have always been sorry that I did not remember the tribe name of the Indians we came in contact with when we first came to the San Joaquin and Kings Rivers. On the San Joaquin around our camp we often heard the name Doo-mah [Dumna]. I am not sure whether that was a tribe name, a name of a chief, or of a village. On Kings River I remember the name Choi-num-ne, but I am also confused in the same way about it.

During the first three years we were on Sycamore Creek, the Indians furnished most of our food. At first we used to hunt and fish a great deal, but we gradually quit it because they used to keep game hanging in the large oak tree in front of the house, and also left their acorn bread at the back door. Most of the time we would never see them do this as they would bring the things while we were gone, or at night while we were asleep. We appreciated this a great deal, as it was a long, hard trip to Stockton after supplies, and we also had very little cash to spend. Several years later I learned from the Indians that they kept us in meat in order to keep us from firing our guns and scaring the game. Of course, we were always good to the Indians and gave them green corn and wheat, but we never in any way came near repaying them for what they did for us.

On the south bank of Kings River, about opposite the mouth of Sycamore Creek, there was an Indian rancheria. There was also another about a mile or two upstream from the first one. These were the people we knew best, and we soon came to know them well, and to trust them completely.

We made a very great distinction between the mountain Indians, or Monaches, and the valley Indians [Yokuts]. Our neighbors at the rancherias belonged to the valley group. Then we later knew the Indians about the north shore of Tulare Lake as lake Indians. I later learned that they belonged to the Tache tribe. Of course, the Telumnes and Wukchumnes around Visalia were valley Indians also, but I did not know them until later and knew very little about them even then.

The valley Indians would not mix with the mountain Indians. They did not talk the same dialect and considered themselves very much better than the Monaches. I knew both tribes quite well, and I believe the valley Indians were justified in their belief. When members of the two groups would meet on a trail they would ignore each other. Some trading was carried on between the two groups, but I am sure it was done by a few members of each group who made a business of it and traveled back and forth between the groups.

On Sycamore Creek we were at about the upstream limits of the valley Indians and the downstream limits of the Monaches. Our territory was really used in common by both groups. They both seemed to travel over it at will, but I believe it was used more by the valley group than by the Monaches.

We soon found that we could not trust the Monaches, and came to consider them as treacherous. Whether they behaved that way toward us because we were friendly with the valley people or not, I do not know. But our neighbors at the rancheria said that the Monaches were thieves and murderers. It is possible that we would have found them all right had we gone directly to them in the first place and not associated with the valley tribes. But it has been my experience that it made no difference how honest Indians may have been within their own tribe, they always considered it their duty to the tribe to do all the damage they could to an enemy, about as the white nations do today.

As I recollect, and I have not been back there for more than seventy years, Sycamore Creek ran between high hills and had only very small patches of level land along it. On these patches my daddy used to raise grain and corn and other crops. This made the work very much scattered, and we had to travel several miles to care for the crops farthest upstream. There were many pools of water in Sycamore Creek, and in them we caught trout and speared a fish we called a steelhead.

Shortly after we settled on Kings River my mother died. It was a terrible blow to all of us and we never realized what she meant to us out there in the wilderness until she was gone. My daddy was gone a great deal of the time, running stock in the valley, and in the mountains. John was riding part of the time for my daddy and part of the time for other settlers who had come to Kings River soon after we had. Ben was old enough to go with either of them, or to look out for himself. But I was younger, and was quite a problem after mother died.

The Indians at the rancheria had always taken an interest in me and I had spent a great deal of time there before my mother died. She was always willing for me to go across the river with them, and I am sure she felt that I was perfectly safe with them.

Sometimes an Indian would come to the edge of the clearing at the back of the house and stand there for hours, looking in the back door and just watching what was going on. We were a whole lot more of a curiosity to them than they were to us, and when we were sure it was one of the valley Indians we paid no attention to him, as we knew that he was just curious to see how we did things. Of course, he would go back to the rancheria and, as I heard them do later when I was living with them, talk for hours to the rest of the Indians about what he had seen. But we never felt safe when the Monaches did that, as they were generally spying out something that they could come back and steal.

Speaking of curiosity reminds me how, when we first came to Kings River, the Indians used to go around after we had planted corn or potatoes and dig up the hills. They did not mean to do any damage, and I believe that in many instances where the white settlers had trouble with the Indians it all started because the Indians were just curious to know what in the world the white settlers were doing and not because they wanted to, or even knew, they were doing any damage.

One of the Indians made me a present of a fine sinew-backed bow of juniper, and a half dozen arrows. This was really as nice a bow as they could get, and was painted in pretty colors. It was about three and one-half feet long, and was made like they made their hunting bows, wide and flat and recurved at the ends, but pinched in or narrowed at the grip. It had been made by one of the Monaches and traded to the people who lived near us.

The Monaches did a lot of fighting and knew how to make good bows. The string was made of sinew and secured at one end by wrapping about the end of the bow. At the other end was a loop which would be slipped up into a nock. The string could be shortened by twisting, or by adjusting at the end opposite the nock.

The valley Indians could not make good bows, as they did not know how to make the waterproof glue with which to fasten the sinew to the back. They really had little use for a bow except for hunting, as they did no fighting among themselves, and there were so many of them that the mountain Indians very seldom bothered them. Then, too, most of their game was caught with snares and traps. They made a crude sort of bow of elderwood without backing and without recurving at the ends. This they used when they could not get the Monache bows.

It is my belief that bow-making, as well as arrow- and bead-making, was understood by only a few individuals, even among the Monaches. I know that they used to take their bows to a certain bow maker in the mountains north of Sycamore Creek to have him repair or replace the sinew backing on them. The Monaches on Sycamore Creek and on Kings River, at least near us, did not know how to do it. I know too, that the Indians passed down most of their arts from father to son and guarded their knowledge so closely that I am sure bow-making was a trade. The word for bow was *drah-lip* and arrow *too-yosh.*

While my folks would have nothing to do with the Monaches, I knew several of them quite well. A few of them could talk the dialect of the valley Indians and I used to talk to them when I met them. They were really better than we thought. By talking to them I came to know many things about them that my folks did not know. I do not believe that many of the other settlers on Kings River knew much about them either.

Shortly after my mother died the Indians at the rancheria held a pow-wow and decided to ask my daddy to let them take me and raise me. So they sent a delegation of five or six women over to our house to talk to my daddy. Of course he immediately said that he would never consent to any such thing. But after a long talk he decided to let me stay with them a few days while he was gone with his stock. When he returned I went back to him, but he was soon gone again. He was later gone so much that I was with the Indians almost continually.

Almost all of the time for more than ten years I was with this tribe of Indians. For at least two different periods of three years each I saw none of my people. This was not strictly true of the second three-year period, because I did see my daddy for about an hour when he rode by one day while the Indians were at Tulare Lake. I will describe that meeting when I tell of our trips to the lake.

While I was at the rancheria I came and went as I pleased. No one of the women claimed me. I was looked after by several of them. They treated me better than they did their own children and probably made a pretty badly spoiled boy of me. I was given the best of everything. They dressed me just as they did their own children while I was small. When I grew older I wore more clothing, generally a breechcloth like the older Indians.

The Choinumne Language

ERY FEW of the Indians I lived with could talk any English. And at that time I could talk no Spanish. But before I went to live with them I had learned some of their dialect and I very soon learned practically all of it.

To me the language of the valley Indians was always interesting. Compared with English, the Indian language I knew was throaty, a series of short syllables, but soft and musical. Many of their words were imitations of the sounds made by the things they were to represent. The word for squirrel was *skée-til*, and was spoken sharply, much as it is barked by the squirrel. The word for the little ground owl, or billy-owl, as we called it, was *péek-ook*, and they bobbed their heads like he does when they said it. If you are close to the billy-owl when he bobs his head you will hear him make a little sound like *péek-ook*. In some tribes the name for ground owl is *wá-tih-te*. Spoken shrilly and sharply, it is an imitation of the screeching call of the ground owl at twilight.

The word for water was *íl-lik* and always reminded me of the sound made by dripping water. The word for deer was *hoey*, and was, I believe, an imitation of the blowing snort of a startled deer. The word for snow was *pun-pun*, the noise your feet make when you walk on loose snow.

The words for ducks and geese were a good deal like the gabbling noise they make when feeding, *wats-wats* and *la-la*. The word for coyote was *ki-yu* and I believe that the Spanish got the word coyote from the Indians.

Another word that might be confused with the Spanish is *cholo*. *Cholo* means white. We call the Spanish, or Mexicans, *cholos*. I believe we did this because when we came here we heard the Indians calling them *cholos*, or whites.

The word for hawk was *swoop*. The word for sleep was *wáwh-yen* and it almost made me yawn to hear them say it.

The Choinumne name for the sun was *óo-push*. The moon they called *áw-push*. When the moon was getting smaller after it became full, they said that a bug was eating it but that the bug always got too full before it ate the moon up and had to stop. Then the moon grew back to its full size again. They recognized an eclipse and said that a coyote was eating the moon or sun. During an eclipse the medicine man used to put on his dance to overcome the coyote's power.

It was always interesting to me that the word *nim*, meaning "mine," was the exact reverse of *min*, meaning "yours." The word for "me" was *nah,* and for "you," *mah.* The word for both niece and nephew was *chi-úhk-nim.* If your meaning was not clear, you had to explain in your sentence just whom you meant. This made Indian language full of repetition.

Winter they called *taw-máw-kish.* Summer was *hi-él.* They did not use words for the other two seasons, spring and fall, that I know. The time when the wild flowers bloomed they called *tish-úm-yu.* I suppose it could be taken to mean spring.

In the spring the Indians were always gathering flowers and fastening them in their hair. If there was patch of wild flowers anywhere near camp, you would see up to a couple of dozen people sitting in them or picking them. Baby-blue eyes were called *lúp-chen súh-suh,* or fish eyes. The tall dark lily *[Brodiaea capitata]* was called *trí-oo.* Another lighter lily *[Brodiaea laxia]* was called *co-lá-we.* Chinese houses were *trá-el-le en-él-o,* or snake's dresses. Our paint brush *[Escobita]* they called *pawtch-áw-le.* Larkspur was called *shíl-cootch.* Blue lupines were *hói-up,* and the California poppy was *shuh-cúg-cuh.* There were dozens of others, but I do not remember them.

Sometimes the sharp tip of a fish gig would be broken off or become dull by striking the gravel in the bottom of the river when they were spearing fish. They called this *hóme-tun,* meaning blunt, or dull, and they would resharpen the point by rubbing the tip on a piece of sandstone. If they broke the tip off an arrow, they used the same word, but they resharpened the arrow point by flaking it with a piece of deer's horn. But they could distinguish between a point that was dull and an edge that was dull. If the edge of an arrow point or a chipped stone knife became dull, they said it was *nih-súh-now*. They sharpened it by chipping with a deer's horn. They used the same word when speaking of a dull steel knife. When the knife was sharp, they said, *"Eén-sheesh háh-nitch,"* meaning "good, sharp." *Hah-nít-lah* meant to sharpen.

There is only one really hard sound to learn in the Choinumne language. It is a sort of an "h" made with a blowing sound, deep in the throat. When a white man tries to yell the letter "h" and blow through his throat at the same time, he loses all his breath before he makes any noise. But an Indian can yell a word with that sound in it so that you can hear it a good half mile. I know a white man can learn this too, because I learned to do it just as well as the Indians.

The words for the four directions had several of these "h's" in them. *K-hú-sheem* was north. West was *t-hú-k-héel*. South was *k-hú-mote*. They often used these words when they were hunting for deer that had been wounded or killed. One Indian would stand on one side of a canyon and yell a half mile to tell another Indian which direction to look for a deer, and he would easily be heard.

I remember that they kept a deer or elk shoulder blade among the cooking utensils and used it for scraping the hardened acorn mush out of baskets and for other jobs like that. They called the bone *top-tóp-ish*. This means leaf-shaped. *Top-top* means leaf. You can see that "ish" means the same as it does in English.

Some other sounds or endings mean the same that they do in other languages, but it is only an accident that they do. I am always reminded of the Scotch word "wee," which we use in English to mean very small. In Indian, *wé-che* means very small. *Wé-ghe* is another word meaning small, but not so small as *wé-che*. *Wé-chet* means little sticks. *Wé-chep* means little child. You can almost always depend that the sound "wee" means something small. The only word I can think of that might be an exception is *we-há-set*, the name for mountain lion. And that might have to do with something about the animal that I do not know about.

When I had been with the Choinumne Indians for about six years, I could talk their language as well as most of the full-blood Indians. I was with them about ten years, and during most of this time I seldom talked anything but Indian. Since I left the Choinumnes in 1862, I have seldom talked any Indian, but I have forgotten very little of the language. Most of it was very easy to learn. It was put together much like English. *He ahm* meant the same as "I am," "you are," "we are," "he is," "she is," or anything of the kind. *He ahm wih-níh-se* might mean "they are ready," "it is ready," or anything of the kind. If there was any chance for confusion, you had to explain by adding more to your sentence.

The Choinumne called the San Joaquin Valley *Chaw-láw-no*. *Wah-áh-hah bah-lú Chaw-láw-no* meant "away down the valley." If an Indian had been gone from the rancheria for an hour and you asked him where he had been, he might say, "*Wah tríp-in.*" That would mean that he had been up the river for a short walk. If he answered, "*Wah-áh-hah tríp-in,*" he would mean that he had gone quite a long distance. If he drew out a long "*Wah-áhhhhh-hah,*" stuck his lips out as far as he could, and pointed his mouth over the hills toward another valley, that would mean that he had been on the longest trip he had ever taken. But the same Indian would sit in the dark and without a motion describe accurately in detail everywhere he had gone, every landmark he had seen on the way. I have sat for hours on summer nights and heard them do this. But it took lots of talking and required the repetition of many words and phrases and even whole sentences.

On the whole, the Indian language I knew was much more cut-and-dried than English. They did not have so many ways of saying a thing as we do. There were not so many words to express the different degrees, colors, or extent of anything. That was why an Indian explained varying distances as I have described.

In general, the Indian words indicated extremes. They had few words to describe the steps in between. The word *háh-pul*, or "hot," was easily understood. So was *tríh-me*, or "cold." But it was hard for them to describe the temperatures in between. Everything was *háh-pul* or *tríh-me*. "Good" was *éen-shesh* and "bad" was *tó-tre*. But it was harder for them than it is for us to describe the degrees of goodness or badness in between. It was the same with the words *drói-ye*, "white," and *múts-ke-wik*, or "black;" with *traw-gáw-nou*, "wet," and *troh-khí-shish*, "dry;" or with *cuh-mó-e*, "all," and *cah-mó-to*, "none."

The word for father was *nó-pope* and for mother, *nó-um*. "Grandmother" was *báh-pish*. "Sister" was *aw-gáwish* and "brother," *ná-bits*. They had enough names so they could name accurately every degree of relationship known to us. There were so many I cannot begin to remember all of them.

The Indians I lived with used the same system of counting that we do. Eleven was ten-one, twelve was ten-two and so on to twenty. Twenty was two-ten, and twenty-one was two-ten-one. Of course they did not use our names for the numbers but used the following:

one	*yá-et* (sounded almost like "yet")
two	*poó-noy*
three	*só-uh-pun*
four	*hóp-poo-noy*
five	*yách-chee-nil*
six	*chú-la-pee*
seven	*núm-chen*
eight	*moó-nosh*
nine	*só-pun-hut*
ten	*tréeo*
eleven	*treeo ya-et*
twelve	*treeo poo-noy*

thirteen	*treeo so-uh-pun*
twenty	*poo-noy treeo*
twenty-one	*poo-noy treeo ya-et*
twenty-two	*poo-noy treeo poo-noy*
thirty	*so-uh-pun treeo*
thirty-three	*so-uh-pun treeo so-uh-pun*
fifty	*yach-chee-nil treeo*
one hundred	*treeo treeo, or ten tens.* Or: *ya-et shinto*

The Indians could count into the millions and keep an absolutely accurate record of any number without writing of any kind. Although *treeo-treeo* meant one hundred, in counting they generally used the word *shinto*. *Ya-et shinto* meant one hundred, *poo-noy shinto* two hundred, and so on to *so-pun-hut shinto*, or nine hundred. One thousand was *ya-et tów-so* (the "ow" sounded as in cow). I know this word sounds like "thousand," and that it may be thought that they got it from the English language, but I am positive that it is not so. I remember that I was on the shore of Tulare Lake with the Indians when a mile-long swarm of wild geese flew over. They actually darkened the sky. One of the old Indians looked up at them and said, "Tow-so tow-so," which to us plainly meant a thousand thousands, or one million. This word was understood by all of the old Indians and I am sure was a part of their own language.

The Indian kept account of his calculations without counters or marks in the sand. I rarely ever saw one count on his fingers. In this sort of calculation the average Indian was much better than the average white man.

I am sure that the above system of counting was not gained from the Spanish, as the Indians had no knowledge of any other, and the real old Indians, with their noses pierced with a long piece of bone and their faces tattooed, used it. These old characters did not use any Spanish words, nor had they taken on any of the white man's customs.

Games

USED TO FIGHT a great deal with the Indian boys and I could whip any of them that were my age. When I would whip one of them his mother and the rest of the women would tease him because he let me get the best of him.

We used to wrestle by the hour. The Indians themselves, even the grown men, used to wrestle a good deal, but were not very good at it. My brother Ben could throw any of them easily.

The Indians used to joke among themselves a good deal, and some of the jokes, especially among the young men, were pretty rough. I remember that when the women were gathering gooseberries and blackberries, they would try to get me to eat many of the other kinds of berries that grew along the river. Some of these were awfully bitter, and some little short of poison, and they would laugh and laugh when I would try to eat some of them.

I used to play many games with the Indian boys and with the grown Indians. The boys used to make dummy ducks, or fish, of bark and throw them in the river. As they floated downstream, we would shoot arrows at them or practice throwing a spear at them. Where the water was shallow we would wade in and recover our weapons. Sometimes we would follow the floating dummy a great distance down the river.

The Indian boys used a sling exactly like the white boys use, but I never saw a grown Indian use one. It was made of buckskin, a piece of skin about three inches square with two strings about two and one-half feet long fastened to it. One string had a loop on the loose end. They placed the loop over one finger and held the end of the other string in the same hand. They gave the sling one fast whirl and let go of the string. The boys liked to see who could throw rocks up the river farthest. I never saw them try to kill anything with a sling. They called it *yó-ketch.*

Each rancheria had a gaming court at, or near, its center. This court was made by smoothing the earth and tamping it solid. It was then covered with fine sand, and many games were played upon it. Here was always an excited, shouting, yelling, laughing group, generally including men, women and children, all intent upon their game and as carefree and happy as it is possible for human beings to be.

The game I remember best was played with a hoop and a pole about ten feet long. They called the game *daw-kói-un.* The pole was about the same size as one of their fish spears. it was called *dáw-koi.* The hoop was made of bark coiled into a flat disc, held together with slender willow shoots, and covered with untanned buckskin. It was called *pahl-wú-sha.* The hoop was about one and one-half feet in diameter and had a hole in the center about two or three inches in diameter.

Any and everyone played this game. Sides were chosen and one person was selected from each side to roll the hoop. These two persons stood about twenty or thirty yards apart and at each end of the game court. They rolled the hoop back and forth between them. The game was to throw a pole through the hoop as it rolled by. For each pole thrown through the hoop, two points were awarded to the side having the lucky, or accurate, player. If the pole passed only partly through and knocked the hoop over, it counted only as one point. The players lined up on each side of the course where the hoop was rolled. They laughed and yelled and made a great deal of noise at this game and did all they could to rattle the opposing players when they were about to throw a pole.

This was a great deal more exciting game that you might think just from reading about it. When the hoop was rolled across the court as many as thirty or forty poles would go flying through the air and the biggest problem in the game was to dodge the poles that came from the other side. They kept the score by calling it aloud much as we keep score in a game of horseshoes.

For another game a small perforated stone was rolled instead of the hoop. This stone was about three or four inches in diameter and had a hole in the center about an inch in diameter. This game was played principally by the young men. It was a much quieter game than the hoop game, but was scored in the same way. They shot wooden pointed arrows at the stone as it passed by. This same stone was used to straighten their arrows and their shafts for gigging fish.

On the same court they used to roll round stones at a hole in the ground and throw flat rocks at a line, but I know very little about the games connected with these practices.

The women had a dice game that was played on a large mat or flat basket. The dice were made of nut shells or acorn caps filled with pitch and decorated on the flat side with small pieces of shell. I have seen them play this game by the hour, but I really knew very little about it. The dice were gathered up in the hand and rolled out on the basket. If two or seven flat sides remained up when the dice had stopped rolling, a point was scored.

The men had a sort of guessing game which they called *ha-nów-ish*. They sat facing each other. One person held two small sticks in his hand, one of which was marked. A pair of these sticks were called *á-sutch*; the blank was *maw-láw-litch*, and the marked one *á-sut*. He would put his hands behind him and shuffle the sticks back and forth from one hand to the other. Finally he would bring his hand to the front closed, and the person opposite attempted to guess in which hand he held *á-sut*, the marked stick. They kept score with small sticks called *wé-chet*. If the one guessing failed to guess the proper hand, he lost to the person holding the stick. If he guessed right, he won a point. The marked stick passed from player to player in rotation.

One of the most amusing games played by the Indians was a sort of football game called *tah-lúh-wush*. A round stone about two or two and one-half inches in diameter was used. This stone was often very round and nicely polished and was known by the name of *tah-luh-wúsh-ee*. The stone was not kicked, but was thrown. The toes were caught under it and it was pushed, or thrown forward. Sides were chosen and goals arranged. Sometimes two trees about two hundred yards apart would be used for goals, or sticks might be planted for goals. They were known as *gó-ish*.

Everyone played, and they surely made a rough-house of it. One person started the ball. A point was scored when the stone was brought in contact with the goal of the opponents. They used to push, shove, hold, trip, and wrestle. Sometimes one side would find that they had one or two more players than the other. Then they would each hold one of the opposite side. This would leave one or two of their players to make a goal unhindered. Sometimes, when the ball was near a goal, both sides would crowd close like a band of milling sheep. Then the ball might come rolling out between the many feet and someone would pass it to the other goal before the mass could break up and stop the play.

A small, round gourd used to grow on the San Joaquin Valley plains. I have seen hundreds of acres of sandy soil along the rivers covered with it. It put out long, tapering, pointed runners with yellow flowers and green gourds, as round as baseballs and slightly larger. Except during the hottest part of the day you would probably see from a half-dozen to forty Indian children playing football with these gourds. Sometimes there would be several games going at one time. They called the gourd *kawl-báw-buh*.

The Indians also played a game exactly like the game of shinny played by white boys today. A wooden ball was used and a club was prepared. This club was curved on one end. This game was scored in the same way as the football game. It was a rough game, and the Indians sometimes were badly bruised in playing it. It was generally played by young men from fourteen to twenty years of age.

Indian Houses and Customs

T HE INDIAN WOMEN did not smoke. The grown men used to smoke very sparingly. They used to make pipes out of the hollow cane *(hala)* that grew along the banks of the streams. These pipes were slender tubes about the diameter of a pencil, and from three to six inches long. They called them *síh-kil.* A few of the older Indians would carry one of these pipes behind their ears and would occasionally light one, take a puff and pass it around. Each person took only one puff. When the puff of smoke was inhaled they held the pipe perpendicular so that the ashes and burning tobacco would not fall out of it. They would inhale deeply and make a blowing sound in their throat as they blew the smoke out. The smoke they called *mo-hó-truk.* To smoke was *báh-moo.* Tobacco they called *dah-áh-goo.*

They did not smoke the leaves of the tobacco, but the seed. The seed was ground up in a mortar. As the tobacco burned, so did the reed pipe, much as the wrapper of a cigarette burns. It was powerful tobacco. I tried a puff or two of it, but it was altogether too strong for me. It was easy for me to understand why they did not smoke more often, or longer at a time. I never saw them use a clay or stone pipe of their own manufacture. The pipe was called *pah-áh-mo.*

The Indians generally married at about the age of twenty years, never at a younger age than fifteen or sixteen. The young man would talk with the parents of the intended bride. Then he would talk to the girl. I rather believe, from one or two things that I saw, that there was often an understanding beforehand between the young man and the intended bride, but I cannot be sure. After the parents of the bride had talked the matter over, and had decided that the young man was all right, they notified him. Then he went away for a short distance, sometimes only a few yards, sometimes a half mile or more, and built a house for his bride.

When the house was finished they started housekeeping. I know of no ceremony, but they said they were *lo-túp-mush* when they married. I am sure that in the tribe that I lived with it was not customary for the new couple to live with either of the parents-in-law. Neither do I know of any taboo against the son-in-law talking to his mother-in-law, as I understand was customary among many of the valley tribes.

The Indians that I knew lived at old Millerton on the San Joaquin River, above Centerville on Kings River, down Kings River to Tulare Lake, and on the north shore of that lake. A person might find that the things I learned from them would not apply to all other tribes in the valley. But I have always thought of them as all being the same people here in the valley. The language of those I knew was almost the same; some words were different, but not very many.

I remember that the name of the head man of the Wukchumnes was called *Wah-táwk-ka*, and that of the lake Indians, or Taches, *Ghee-górío*. Another Indian I knew quite well was called *Koo-táh-mah*.

There was considerable difference between the houses built by different tribes. On Tulare Lake a long house was built of a thin layer of tules, but on [upper] Kings River quite a permanent building was constructed. They would dig a hole in the ground to a depth of as much as two feet. This hole would be about circular, and from ten to twenty feet in diameter. The soil was loosened with pointed sticks and carried out in baskets. The soil removed was thrown out around the sides of the hole. Then the butts of long, slender willow poles would be planted in the bottom of this hole, next to the walls. These poles would be placed about six inches apart.

A space about two feet wide was left for a door at the south side of the house. A willow hoop about two and one-half feet in diameter was made. The tops of the poles were bent together at the top and tied to the hoop. Then more long, slender poles were bent around the outside of the upright poles and tied to them about two feet apart. This made a beehive-shaped wickerwork frame. Around and over this frame were stood tules to a depth of about ten or twelve inches. Then the soil was thrown over the tules to a depth of several inches. I remember the word for tules was *sói-yoo*.

After a few years the grass grew over the house and it looked like an underground house, or cellar. In bad weather the fire was kindled in the middle of the house under the round hole which had been left at the top. Some of the smoke found its way out through the hole above. There was no other opening except the door.

The house was used only in bad weather except for sleeping. Otherwise cooking and eating and all preparation of materials would be carried on outside. The floor of the house would be covered with several thicknesses of tule mats. Around the inside of the wall tule mats would be piled up to a thickness of several inches. These served as a mattress for sleeping. When they could be obtained, grizzly bear skins were used on top of the mattress. In very cold weather a rabbit skin blanket would be used in addition to the bear skin. They called the blanket *chih-cú-nah.* Then, too, in cold weather some of the old people would be up most of the night rebuilding the fire, which they called *oo-sóot.* When I awakened I would see them moving quietly about and sometimes talking to each other in low tones. The common house was called *tráh-ehv;* the sweat house, *maws.*

Near the house there was generally a shallow pit in which a fire was kept burning most of the time. In the evenings or during cold weather they would sit about it rather than go in the house. They were outside almost all of the time. All of the camp refuse was thrown in the fire pit. When an Indian washed his face and hands he would go to the fire and stand there until he was dry. They used no towels, and none were necessary when the skin was dried by the fire immediately. *Shoom-lŭ-suh* was "to wash."

The Indians did not eat at regular hours, except possibly the evening meal. They had no lamps and they made it a practice to have all their work done and their last eating done about sundown. The hunters would come in shortly before that time and generally everyone would gather around for a meal. This evening meal they called *caw-náw-she.*

In the morning, after the dip in the river, the population of an Indian rancheria generally scattered. The men would visit all of their traps and snares to see what had been caught during the night. Even the small boys would have snares set.

Some of the men would go hunting, some fishing, and some to work on things that they might be making. Some of the women would go into the hills after roots and other materials for weaving or basketry, or along the river to gather berries, or on the plains and hills to harvest seeds. Gradually everyone would wander back to the rancheria late in the forenoon. They would eat in turn as they wandered in. They called this forenoon meal *wah-áh-lut.*

Choinumne Cooking

HE INDIANS ALWAYS had a supply of food stored up. An Indian might go out and hunt all morning, or all day, and not get any game, but he could always come home and get something to eat.

Lots of wild oat seed was prepared and eaten each year. This was an important food to the Choinumnes. The seed was gathered with a basket and a fan-shaped wicker seed-beater. The woman held the basket in the hollow of her left arm and the seed-beater in her right hand. She walked about among the oats, holding the basket below the heads with the mouth sloping forward. With the seed-beater she thrashed the seed into the basket. Many other seeds were gathered in the same way.

The oats were stored in baskets and skin bags and prepared as they were needed. They were generally parched on a flat tray. Hot rocks or coals were put on the tray with the oats. The tray was shaken until the spike and fur covering was burned from the seed, and the seed itself was browned. The seed was then winnowed and looked a lot like wheat that was badly shrunken.

Sometimes they parched the oats and other seeds in stone mortars. I have seen them parch them in iron kettles they obtained from the whites. The parched seed was pounded in a mortar and was cooked in a basket with water and hot rocks to form a gruel or mush much like acorn mush. Their name for wild oat mush was *haw-áw-nus*. I suppose they used the same word for the plant itself, but I am not sure.

Inside the house would be stored acorns, dried fish, dried game, dried grasses, and many kinds of seeds. Outside was an acorn granary, called *solé-nuh*. The acorns themselves they called *pó-in*. The granary was built to hold many bushels of acorns and was used only at permanent villages. Four poles about ten or fifteen feet long were planted in the ground in the form of a square about four feet across. Around these were woven willow shoots. A bottom was woven into the sides about two feet from the ground. The inside of this wicker frame was lined with tules or a grass which the squirrels did not like. The acorns were poured in at the open top from the baskets in which they had been carried from the hills. When some acorns were wanted from the granary the grass would be pulled apart near the bottom and the acorns would run out into a basket. They would then be carried to a shady place to be hulled.

It was really a lot of work to prepare acorns for use. The women did all of this. First they gathered them in the timber and filled their tall, cone-shaped baskets with them. They fitted a net made of milkweed string around this basket. To this net was fastened a long strap woven of milkweed string. The basket full of acorns was placed on the back and the strap passed around in front of the forehead. Occasionally a small basket was worn over the head under the strap, but many times nothing of the sort was used. In this way the acorns were carried as far as two or three miles to the granary.

The acorns were hulled on a large, flat rock in the shade by the stream. They were stood on end on the rock and the top struck with another rock. The dry hull would crack open and fall away. In the large, flat rock were many holes where the hulled acorns were ground into flour. A few hulled acorns were thrown into one of these holes, or mortars, and pounded with a long, slender rock, or pestle. The flour was brushed from the mortar with a brush made of soaproot husk, and placed in a sort of sieve, or colander, made of fine willow shoots. In this it was sifted and the coarse particles returned to the mortar.

Next a hollow basin about a foot or more across was made in the sand by the stream. The acorn flour was mixed with water and pounded into this basin. Then several basketfuls of hot water were poured over it. The hot water carried the bitterness from the flour down into the sand below. The wet flour was then allowed to stand until it had dried into a large cake. When dry it was lifted from its bed and the sand brushed from it. In this condition it was used as bread, which the Indians called *shấh-shah.*

From the acorn bread was made a sort of acorn soup, or gruel *(tíh-pin).* The bread was pulverized and mixed with a large quantity of water. This was all heated. All cooking such as boiling was done in baskets. These baskets were made by the women and were watertight. They had very pretty designs woven into them. Rocks were heated in the fire and dropped into a basket of water or soup. These rocks were called *poh-có-yen.* A looped stick, called *shí-ow,* was used to handle the rocks and to stir the contents of the basket. This stick was made of an oak limb about one-half inch in diameter and four or five feet long. It was doubled in the middle and the two ends fastened together. A small loop was left at the other end. The hot rocks would be caught between two green sticks and lifted into the basket. Then the contents of the basket would be stirred with the looped end of the stick. When the heat had passed from the rock it was again caught in the loop and replaced in the fire.

The only cooking or kitchen utensils I ever saw the Indians use were baskets and mortars. They used small baskets for dippers, and around camp they drank from them.

The Indians kept most of their belongings in baskets and in bags. Their word for basket was *ấh-mut;* for bag it was *kísh-tul.* Most of their bags were made by gathering up the edges of an irregularly shaped piece of elk or buckskin and tying a string around it. They made them from a size that would hold a hundred pounds of acorns down to a size they could hold in the palm of the hand.

They had many kinds of baskets. They made a sort of colander of cottonwood twigs, which they called *cháh-pi*. An almost flat winnowing tray was called *po-múh-nuh*. The large cooking baskets were called *tún-ah*. A large, cone-shaped carrying basket was called *áh-nush*. A small basket for a drinking cup was called *áh-mutch*. A basket cap to wear on the head under the burden strap was called *wó-wee*. The women had a large, flat tray that they played a dice game on. They called it *tí-won*. Most of these baskets had very pretty designs on them, almost every kind of a design you could think of. When they were soaked in water they would not leak, and they were almost as strong as though they were made of sheet iron.

When there was an acorn shortage the seed of the buckeye was prepared and eaten. These were poisonous and the meal had to be leached much longer than the acorn flour. The leaves of the manzanita were also powdered and mixed with the buckeye flour and helped to reduce the bitterness. Otherwise the buckeye bread was prepared the same as the acorn bread. The manzanita berry was also eaten, but both it and the buckeye were always eaten with clover, greens, or other laxatives, the use of which the Indians well understood.

A sweet cider was made from the juice of the manzanita berries. They were crushed in mortars and set in wicker colanders to drain into baskets. A little water was added to the crushed berries. This made a sweet and well-flavored cider, and I remember it with more relish than anything I ever ate or drank with the Indians.

They ate great quantities of young tule roots, which were soft and sweet. The lake Indians made an almost pure starch from tule roots. The women waded into the water and dug the roots out with pointed sticks. Other women pulled the roots out onto the bank. There the women cut the roots from the stalks.

The roots were thrown into stone mortars and were pounded into a soft mass. The pounded roots were then thrown into a large cooking basket and were covered with hot water. The mixture was stirred with the looped stirring stick for an hour or so. Then the crushed roots were raked out and were thrown away. In an hour or two, the starch had settled to the bottom of the basket. The water was then poured off. They obtained in this way a cake of starch two inches in thickness, and eight or nine inches in diameter. It had very little taste but was very rich. They also ate the tule roots, which tasted like slippery elm.

At Tulare Lake, great quantities of grass nuts were gathered and eaten. These were not the bulbs of the wild flowers, but grew underground in the sandy places, particularly about the lake. They had a bunch of stickers on the top and a sort of husk or hull on them, and grew on a long root, like beads on a string. The hull was black and the nut sweet and rich. The Indians also ate the bulbs of the wild flowers, and when the stems of the flowers had dried the women would go out over the hillsides and dig them by the bushel.

The Indians would not eat a coyote. I never knew why, but I am sure there was some reason for it.

Pine nuts were eaten in great quantities. The Indians called them *tawn*. After two or three hundred pounds of pine burrs had been gathered, they were piled up and fired. The burrs were covered with pitch, called *cháh-ki*, and this made them burn easily. The Indians called the pine burrs *shúm-shoom*. It was almost impossible to remove the nuts in any other way. They were covered with sharp spines and were so solid that they could not be opened with anything the Indians had. The coating of pitch also made them hard to handle. I have always figured that the pitch was a part of the effort of nature to keep squirrels and other pests away from the nuts. After the outside of the burrs had been burned a little, they began to curl open and the nuts would become loose. The Indians would use a stick to rake the burrs out of the fire and knock the nuts out. Finally they would have a pile of about fifteen or twenty pounds of nuts for their trouble. These they cracked and ate as they were, partly roasted. Some of the nuts they would mash and make into mush. This mush was very rich, and a person could eat only a small amount of it.

Everyone—men, women and children—might eat at the same time and together. They all ate from the same basket, dipping the food out with the three first fingers of the right hand, but they generally ate when they felt hungry and generally ate alone.

Indians were very careful about polluting a stream near their rancheria or camp. If they had to wade the stream they would do so below the camp, or they might cross on rocks above. The sweat house was located below camp and all bathing was done there. They would very seldom wash their hands and face in a stream. When drinking from a stream they would arise with their mouths full of water. They would allow this water to run over their hands and would in that way wash their hands and faces away from the stream. One mouthful of water would wash hands and face and leave some to spare. To wash was *shoom-lú-suh*.

When rock salt could be obtained, it was used for seasoning, but to me it tasted more like alum than salt. The Choinumne used in its stead a salt stick. The bark was peeled from a small willow limb. This limb was whipped about in the salt grass that grew in great quantities. On the leaves of the salt grass were many small particles of sticky salt. A coating of this salt, which they called *áh-lit*, was accumulated on the stick. In the field this stick was attached to the gee string. The Indians would pull a handful of sweet clover, roll it into a ball between the palms of their hands, and stuff it into their mouths. Then after it had been chewed, the salt stick was drawn through the mouth. They also ate mustard, which they called *trúhm-ul*, miner's lettuce, and many other greens, both raw and cooked. The salt from the salt grass was dried and was also used for seasoning. It had a sour, salty taste, a good deal like a dill pickle.

Mineral salt was highly valued by the Choinumne and had to be obtained in trade from the Paiutes, who got it by boiling down the waters of Owens Lake. They filled a basket with lake water, heated rocks and held them in the water until cool. This they continued until a cake of mineral salt was obtained about the size of a soup plate.

Small game was roasted in the ashes and coals, leaving the skin on. When the meat was done the skin would be stripped off and the squirrel or quail would be as clean and nice as you would want it. *Chúh-ki él-ish* meant to roast in the ashes and coals. Many times the entrails were eaten. They were split open and washed and stewed or broiled over the coals.

Meat was broiled on the end of a long, slender withe. The big end of the withe would be set in the ground at some distance from the fire, and the meat hung on the other end. The weight of the meat bent the withe over until the meat hung directly over the fire, or coals. In this way the heat from the fire would not burn the withe. The Choinumne word for broil was *chíh-kill.*

After the evening meal they would all lie around the fire on the ground through the long evening and tell stories and sing until as late as ten or eleven o'clock. This was the finest part of their lives. Here was the real family circle. The long evenings were spent about the fires in the most pleasant way imaginable. Every night was a bonfire party. The old sages would tell stories about their own experiences when they were young, or about the history of their tribe, or just simple stories they may have made up. We youngsters would sit around with our mouths and eyes and ears open and listen until we had to go to bed.

Three musical instruments were used, sometimes all at once, and sometimes as an accompaniment to singing. They used a sort of flute made of a hollow elder limb. This made a shrill, whistling sound. They called it *ó-trut*.

They had a clapper made of a split stick, called *trów-ul*. They struck this against something in time to the flute. Instead of the clapper they sometimes beat on a section of log with any stick that came handy. I believe that some of these logs were hollow, or had been hollowed out on the under side.

Probably the best-sounding musical instrument was a short bow, called *máh-way*. It was smaller than their hunting bow and was not recurved at the ends. They placed one end of the back of this against their teeth and thumbed the string like one would a guitar, raising and lowering the pitch with the mouth much as a jews harp is played. This music used to accompany their singing. Some of their songs were quite monotonous, but some of them were very pretty. In general, however, I would much rather read about Indian music than listen to it. I remember that they used to get started on three or four notes that suited them and just play those notes over and over, until it seemed that they would never stop. I never heard the Indians whistle except in signaling to one another.

When the men were hunting they sometimes used to go along with their bows strung and play them in the same way as they did the musical instrument, using an arrow to strike the string.

As the evening wore on, and various individuals grew tired or sleepy, they would wander off to bed. We would go inside and lie down on the tule mattresses next to the walls of the house with our feet to the fire and cover up with a rabbit skin blanket, or whatever the weather demanded. We slept in the clothing we had been wearing during the day, which consisted of a breechcloth and a gee string. We had no shoes or other clothing to take off unless the weather was extremely cold, when we might have a wild cat or mountain lion skin about our shoulders.

Fishing and Hunting

HE INDIANS on the San Joaquin and Kings Rivers used to catch fish with a pointed net made of milkweed string and fastened to a willow hoop. This they set in the river with the mouth upstream. To it they added wings of willow wicker construction. Then they drove the fish downstream into the net.

The Indians trapped lots of fish. They built the trap of small, green limbs. It had wings extending to each side of the river and was located just below a riffle. Between the wings was a hole. In the deep water below and connected to the hole was a long, basket-like trap. It was about three feet in diameter and eighteen or twenty feet long.

The Indians would go upstream from the trap and build a sort of drag to scare the fish down into the trap. They tied oak limbs end to end until they reached across the river. Then they tied the butts of brush to the oak limbs. The fish could not get through the brush.

When the drag was completed, the Indians would pull on each end of the oak limbs and draw the affair downstream. The current would help force it down to the trap. The brush would comb the fish out of the holes. When they arrived at the riffle, the fish could be seen flopping over into the trap. The trap would be filled almost solid with fish. They would catch hundreds in one drive.

Some of the fish they would eat fresh, and some they would dry. Not a fish went to waste. They would fasten the trap to the bank and keep some of the fish in it and eat them fresh for a long time.

They also caught fish in pools with a wicker basket. This

basket was three feet or more in diameter at the large end, about eighteen inches high, and eight inches across the small end, which was left open. They would wade quietly in a pool until they could see a fish. Then they would clap the basket, large end down, over it. The fish thus trapped would be removed by reaching through the small open end of the basket. They would bite the top of the head off the fish and throw it out on the bank.

Trout and other large fish were speared with a gig called *tó-coi*, which was almost like a modern salmon gig. It had a long, slender pole for a handle. This pole was made of elderberry wood, often twenty feet long and about an inch in diameter. It would be as straight as an arrow, and as smooth as glass. Fishermen took a great deal of pride in the fish gigs and would keep them polished until they were shiny.

On the larger end of the pole they would fit two short, sharp pieces of hardwood or bone. One of these was lashed on one side of the big end of the pole, and projected beyond the end of the pole about four inches. It was called *gée-bish*. The other piece was shorter and was blunt on the end. It was lashed opposite the first, making the two projecting pieces about an inch apart.

On the blunt end of the second piece was fitted, by means of a socket, a short, sharp piece of bone or hardwood, called *hó-chesh*. It was attached to the pole by means of a string through a hole near the middle. This string had several inches of slack in it and was called *hé-loo*. When the fish was speared, the unjointed tip would pull out, and the socketed tip would be disengaged and would turn crossways inside of the fish. The fish was then attached to the end of the pole with a short piece of string and could be hauled in without any danger of breaking the gig with its struggling. I believe that the unjointed point was necessary in order to keep the other point from slipping off the fish.

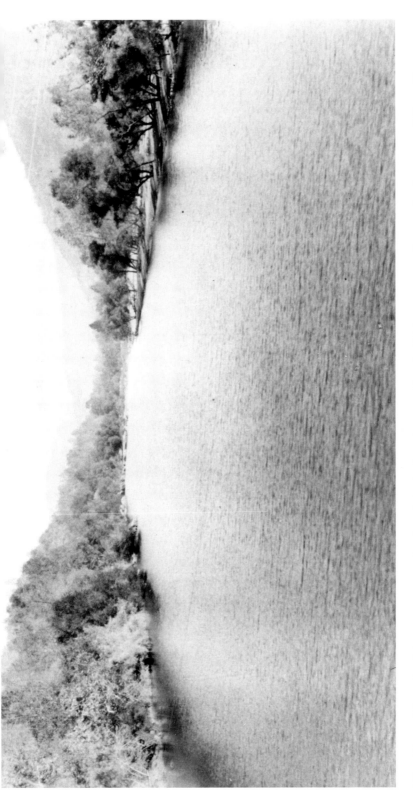

The Kings River, looking upstream. At the right is the site of the Choinumne village where Mayfield lived. On the opposite bank, hidden by trees, is the mouth of Sycamore Creek. This area now lies at the bottom of Pine Flat Reservoir. *Photo by Frank F. Latta, courtesy of Yosemite National Park Research Library*

Opposite, above: Two immense valley oaks
near Porterville, a remnant of the great oak
forests that once occupied the deltas of the
Kings River, the Kaweah River, and other
rivers that flowed into Tulare Lake. *Photo by
Jeff Edwards*

Opposite, below: The valley of the Kaweah
River. Note the almost unbroken forest of
oaks. Drawing by Charles Koppel, 1853.
*Courtesy of Bancroft Library, University of
California, Berkeley*

Below: The San Joaquin River as it flows out
of the Sierra at Fort Miller, where the
Mayfield family tried unsuccessfully to mine
for gold. 1853. *Courtesy of Bancroft Library,
University of California, Berkeley*

VALLEY OF THE SAN JOAQUIN AT FORT MILLER.

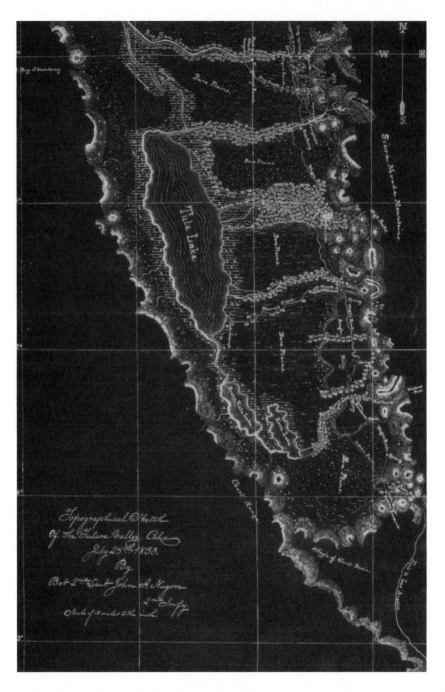

Map of Tulare Lake and the rivers that flow into it, by John Nugen, 1853. Note the size of the lake, the areas of swamp, of oak forest, and of bare plains. A slight rise to the north of the lake prevents the water from flowing north except during flood years when the waters flow through the slough into the San Joaquin River. *Courtesy of Bancroft Library, University of California, Berkeley*

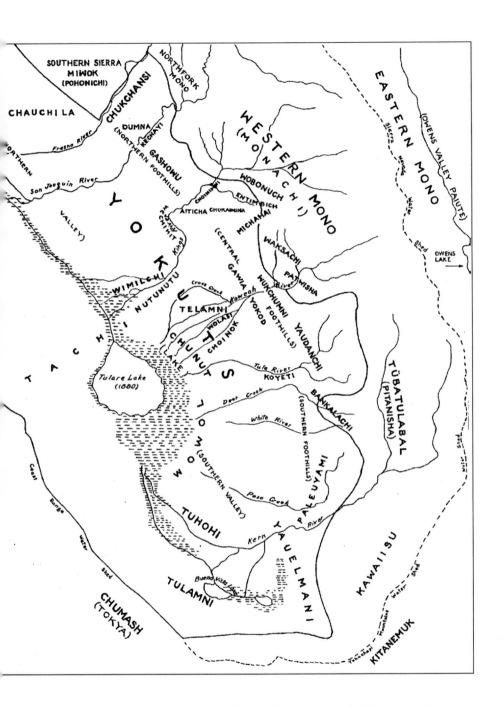

Map of the Indian groups of the southern San Joaquin Valley done by anthropologist Anna Gayton, 1948, based largely on a previous map by Alfred Kroeber. The Yokuts groups are shown in some detail, while the surrounding peoples—Chumash, Kawaiisu, Tubatulabal, Western Mono, and Southern Sierra Miwok—are more roughly indicated.

California rancheria des Indiens d'hockt surls bord de la rivière de la plum

Top: Yokuts village sketched by F. Wikersheim, probably in the 1850s. Note the acorn granaries among the houses and the western-style shirts hung out to dry. *Courtesy of Bancroft Library, University of California, Berkeley*

Bottom: Pigeon blind. Photo copyright 1924 by Edward S. Curtis. *Courtesy of National Anthropological Archives, Smithsonian Institution*

Top: "Summer house" at Tulare Lake, 1903. *From the C. Hart Merriam Collection, courtesy of the Bancroft Library, University of California, Berkeley*

Bottom: "The Plain between the San Joaquin and Kings Rivers." Horses had escaped from the Spanish missions near the coast and by the time of the gold rush had become well established. Drawing by Charles Koppel, 1853. *Courtesy of the Bancroft Library, University of California, Berkeley*

Below: Mono girls swimming, 1904. *Photo by Nellie McGraw, courtesy of Joel Hedgpeth*

Above: Yokuts man in small tule canoe at Ventura County Fair. *Photo by John P. Harrington*

Left: Basketry among the Yokuts was a highly developed art form, with some baskets woven so tightly they could hold water. Note the rattlesnake design and the feathers. *Photo courtesy of Phoebe Apperson Hearst Museum of Anthropology*

Above: Bedrock mortar holes with pestles, used by Yokuts women to pound acorns and seeds. *From the C. Hart Merriam Collection, courtesy of the Bancroft Library, University of California, Berkeley*

Right, top: Wukchumne woman, Maggie Icho, demonstrating traditional Yokuts cooking, 1945. She is using the long "tongs" to drop a hot rock into a cooking basket. *Photo courtesy of the Southwest Museum*

Right, bottom: Maggie Icho removing a hot rock from a cooking basket using a looped stirring stick, 1945. *Photo courtesy of the Southwest Museum*

Below: Yokuts women gambling with walnut dice and specially made gambling trays. *Photo courtesy of Bancroft Library, University of California, Berkeley*

Below: Group of Indians at Tejon. *Courtesy of Yosemite National Park Research Library*

Left: Indian women in downtown Visalia (not dated). *Photo courtesy of Yosemite National Park Research Library*

Below: The Pullow'oo family, Choinumne, 1903. *From the C. Hart Merriam Collection, courtesy of the Bancroft Library, University of California, Berkeley*

Right, top: Card tables at the Mitchell Hotel, Tailholt, 1898. Thomas Jefferson Mayfield is the man with the black coat and black hat seated at the table on the right. *Photo courtesy of Yosemite National Park Research Library*

Right, bottom: Mayfield, left, with two other early settlers, Zac Blankenship and Frank Bequette, all over eighty, 1928. Photo by Frank Latta. *Courtesy of Yosemite National Park Research Library*

Below: Mayfield in front of an old cabin in Tailholt, 1928. Photo by Frank Latta. *Courtesy of Yosemite National Park Research Library*

Frank Latta in his Baker Electric with a
Yokuts man identified as Johnnie Garcia,
1946. *Photo by Forbes, courtesy of Yosemite
National Park Research Library*

In using the gig they built a sort of scaffolding over the water. A deep place in the stream was selected and two long poles were set on end ten or fifteen feet from the bank. These poles, which were about ten feet apart at the bottom, crossed at the top about level with the bank. Where they crossed, they were lashed together. Then the ends of two more long poles would be placed in the crotch above where the first two poles crossed, with the other ends resting on the bank about ten feet apart. This formed two v-shaped arrangements with the points of the v's together, the open part of one on the bed of the stream and the open part of the other on the bank.

Across the horizontal poles were laid smaller poles and branches to make a dense shade. The fisherman lay on his stomach on top of the branches and dropped the point of the gig down through an opening in them. When the fish passed into the shade below, it could be seen and was promptly gigged.

Ground squirrels were quite plentiful and, as I have mentioned before, in some places the ground was cast up into great mounds by them. The Indians used to kill these squirrels by smoking them out. A party of a dozen or more of the men would go out on the plains for a squirrel hunt. They would select one of the large dens where there were hundreds of squirrels. They would fill the tops of all the holes in a large den with earth, except four or five of the main ones. Then they would stuff grass and weeds in the open holes and set fire to them. A basket or skin would be used to fan and force the smoke into the holes.

After the holes had been filled with smoke the ones through which the smoke had been forced would be filled. Then the parties who had been doing the smoking would sit down in the shade for a couple of hours and sleep, or play their guessing game. If they were near the river, sometimes they would fish.

When the holes were opened, the squirrels would be found dead near the top, where they had tried to get out to the fresh air. The hunters would tuck the heads of the squirrels under their gee strings, which were tied tightly around their waists. Sometimes all of the hunters would have a complete girdle of squirrels. I remember seeing them come in that way many times when I was very young, and later I hunted squirrels with them. Ground squirrels were almost the best and the most unfailing of their food sources.

They trapped quail in a wicker basket by means of a low fence. The basket, shaped like a fly trap turned flat on the ground, was placed at an opening in the fence. The quail would run along the fence rather than fly over it and would enter the basket through the opening.

There was quite a variety of food for the Indians to eat. In addition to the things I have already mentioned were mud hens, ducks, geese, larks, sandhill cranes, swans, rabbits, raccoons, antelope, elk, deer, gophers, many kinds of roots and seeds, and other things of minor importance.

The Indian families were comparatively small, three to four children, rarely as many as five. So it was comparatively easy for the head of the family to provide game, and for the woman to gather plenty of seeds and acorns.

Native Wild Life

THERE WERE ABOUT six kinds of geese in the San Joaquin when I first came here, and there were probably billions of them. I have seen the white geese with black wing tips flying so thickly that I am positive one band of them would cover four square miles of land as thick as they could land and take off again. The Indians trapped these geese at Tulare Lake, but I never saw it done. I like to hunt antelope, elk, coons and deer better than to hunt any kind of water fowl or to fish, but I have seen forty Indians come in from the swamps at one time, loaded down with all of the white geese they could carry. I have also seen the nets the Indians used to catch geese and ducks, but I know nothing about them, except that they were made of string, were tied something like a fish net, and were fastened to light willow poles. They called the white geese *gául-tut*. The speck-led-breasted goose was called *gú-soose*. I believe that I have forgotten the names of all the other kinds of geese. I do remember that the Indians called the mud hen *táh-cha*.

The word *wáts-wats* meant mallard duck, but it was used for all ducks when it made no difference. The teal duck was called *cú-ee*. The wood duck, which nested in hollow trees and was the most beautiful bird in the country, was called *bo-wíl-nah*.

The word for blackbird was *chock*, almost identical with the word for skunk. The small, common blue jay was called *chí-chee*. There was a larger, crested jay that lived in the higher mountains. They called it *khí-khe*. "Condor" was *wíh-itch*, and "buzzard" was *hawts*. The name for blue bird was *jo-jó-ill*, and for blue fish crane, *wáh-cut*. The sandhill crane they called *wáh-h*. The word had a short of "h" sound tacked on the end. The bald eagle was sacred to the Choinumne. They called it *tró-q-hill.* The black eagle was called *háw-toy.* Crow was *áhl-woot.* The large, red-tailed chicken hawk was an important bird. The medicine men used the down from the breast of this bird the same as they did from the eagle. They called the hawk *swú-hoop* and got this word the same way we got our word "swoop." They had a name for every bug or bird or animal that walked or crawled or hopped or flew, and every grown Indian knew every one of them.

There used to be a sort of fish in Tulare Lake that must have been an eel. It looked like pictures I have seen of eels. The Indians called it *ká-wus ká-wus.* One kind of trout was called *dów-wish,* a fish having a yellowish tinge. Steelhead trout were called *á-pis.* Suckers were called *púl-khwee* and salmon *khí-khit.* The general word for any kind of fish was *ló-put.*

The Indians often had pet deer around camp. They would capture fawns and feed them on acorn soup and keep them around camp until they were grown or until the first mating season, and then they would seldom be seen again. The word for fawn was *chá-wik;* for doe, *nó-oom;* and for buck, *i-kéel.*

The Indians had always had dogs. Although this may seem strange, I am positive I am right. Their name for dog was *chá-shish.* When I was with the Indians on the upper Kings River (1850), they still had some dogs that they claimed had not been mixed with white man's dogs. These were about as big as, but heavier than an average coyote, and were about the same color. Their hair was shorter and thicker. Their ears were not so erect, and their noses not so pointed. They could easily have been mistaken for coyotes. The Choinumne word for the bark of a dog was *wáh-hoo.* I have heard many white people use exactly that same call when they were trying to attract the attention of someone at a distance.

Many of the white people thought that there were five kinds of bears in the mountains. They thought there were two kinds of grizzlies, one a silvertip, which was nothing more than the common grizzly with his full winter coat. Then they thought there were brown, black and cinnamon bears. The Indians observed everything about them too closely ever to be deceived about such things. They knew that the last three bears came from the same mother. They had just two words: *náw-hawn* for grizzly and *mo-hó-o* for black bear.

I knew the Choinumne names for all of the animals, but I suppose I have forgotten all but the common ones. "Antelope" was *súey-all*, "porcupine" was *pów-putch*, and "badger" was *trúh-now*. The Indians were always interested in bats and had many stories about them, but I did not learn them. The children who ran with me around the rancheria used to hunt for bat roosts and capture the bats. The name for bat was *sím-sim*, and was an imitation of the squeak made by them. The name for beaver was *tá-pik*. The golden mantle squirrel was called *tih-wíh-che* and the chipmunk, which is smaller but looks like the squirrel, was called *ghig-wíl-itch*. The way the Indians pronounced these words was a good imitation of the sounds the animals made. "Cottontail" was *tá-o* and "jackrabbit" *hó-moke*.

The name for elk was *shúck-quoy*, and for fox was *ów-ih-chuh,* meaning a person who makes an "ow" noise. There was another fox, a very small fox which lived in holes out on the San Joaquin plains. They called it *soom*. Mink was called *nah-hí-etch*, "raccoon" was *kíd-chee* and "wild cat" *táw-nul*. "Gray squirrel" was *mow* and "wolf" *e-wáy-it*. There were dozens of others, but I have probably forgotten most of them.

The Indians always imagined that bad, mean animals were in the woods, imaginary ones that no one ever saw. Young people liked to scare each other, especially at night. They used the word *peesh* to indicate these imaginary beasts. After I had been gone from the Indians for ten years, I would still jump out of my skin if anyone yelled *"peesh!"* behind me in the dark woods.

Hunting Lore

T HE INDIAN did not hold his bow like a white man does. It was short and was held diagonally. The arrow was placed on top of the bow, which would be opposite to the method used by modern archers. I believe that this was because they stalked much of their game and a long bow, or one held perpendicularly, would be seen too easily.

An Indian could shoot from cover without exposing more than the point of the arrow and one eye. He turned his head to one side and sighted along the top of the arrow. The string was drawn by the first two fingers of the right hand and the arrow was pinched between them. The fingers on the string were not held straight. The tips were doubled inward and the string rested on the ends of them. As the arrow was released, the fingers were snapped to a straight position. In drawing a very heavy bow, three fingers would be used. The bow was not drawn back and held any length of time while aim was being taken, but was drawn back quickly and released quickly in a sort of snap shot.

An Indian hunter was always cranky about anyone handling his bows or arrows. He kept his bow in a case, called *loh-trów-e*, made of the skin from a mountain lion's tail. The arrows were kept in a fox skin quiver with the head down and the tail left on. It was hung on the Indian's back by a loop made of the skin of the hind legs and was called *mó-hote*. When the bow and arrows were not in use, they were hung on forked sticks high up in the Indian house or in the brush shade they used on the plains. No Indian would think of handling his weapons until he was ready to go hunting, and after he had sweated and bathed.

I remember that sometimes white settlers or cattlemen would come to camp. They would always want to take down every bow they saw and string it and shoot it. They were always clumsy at it, and would damage the arrows and sometimes break the bow. But that was not the real reason the Indians were touchy about having their weapons handled.

The Indians shot most of their game from a distance of less than fifty feet. If possible, an Indian hunter would shoot deer at a range of from twenty to thirty feet. He seldom fired an arrow that did not hit the deer in a vital place. No white hunter could get that close to a deer, because the deer would scent him. Few white people knew how the Indian was able to get that close.

Before going on a deer hunt, the Indian went into the sweat house, called *maws*, and sweated for an hour, wearing his breechcloth. Then he ran and jumped into the water and washed himself off thoroughly. For several hours after such a bath, an Indian had no scent that a deer could smell. Now, there was no use in the Indian's going to all that trouble if his bow and arrows were going to carry the scent of a man. So he did not touch them until after he had come from his bath.

The Indians knew that smoke would kill the scent of a hunter. So, if one of them wanted to go hunting in a hurry, he would throw some weeds in the fire pit and stand in the smoke and turn round and round in it for a few minutes before he took down his bow and arrows. The effect of this was only good for about an hour and was of very little use in hunting deer, because deer were almost as afraid of fire or smoke as they were of a man.

Of course, the Indians knew dozens of things about the habits and likes and dislikes of deer that white men never even suspected. They also watched the direction of the wind very closely, and could call to them almost every game bird or animal in the hills.

When I was quite young, the Indians used to kill many deer by stalking and shooting them with the bow and arrow. For this sort of hunting, they prepared the horns and hide of the deer and placed them over themselves. The head of the deer was hollowed out and was fitted over the head of the hunter. The skin covered the back of the hunter. A short stick was carried in the right hand and was used to imitate the forelegs of a deer when the hunter bent forward. The bow and arrows were carried in the left hand. He would imitate a deer feeding and rubbing his horns on the brush, and many other actions of the deer, until he approached quite close to the game. Sometimes the hunter would work an hour to get just ten feet closer to the deer.

The Indians also killed a good many deer by surrounding them. They called this kind of hunting *trah-nów-shish*. A hundred or more Indians would surround a deer in a thicket. Then two or three men with bows and arrows would go into the thicket. The Indians on the outside would yell and beat the brush and make enough noise to be heard two or three miles. The deer would be so badly scared that it didn't know which way to run. Finally, one of the men with a bow and arrows would get a shot at close range and kill the deer.

The Indians I lived with used arrows tipped with obsidian and also arrows tipped with hardwood. They were made with a socketed foreshaft. They also made a one-piece arrow for use in practicing. A good, straight arrow shaft was of more value to them than a point. By making the arrow of two pieces, they could remove a damaged point and place a good one on the shaft in a few seconds. In this way, there was no necessity for carrying more than three or four shafts. Any number of foreshafts could be carried rolled in moss and buckskin.

In the two-piece arrows the shaft was fitted with a socket in the fore end. When game was shot with an arrow, the foreshaft and the point remained in the flesh, even though the animal rubbed against the tules or brush and pulled off the shaft. This was also an advantage in warfare, as the arrow could not be entirely removed without leaving a bad wound. If an arrow missed the game and the point was damaged by striking a rock, the shaft could be fitted with a new foreshaft and point and was ready for use immediately.

Obsidian-tipped arrows were used in warfare and in killing large game. For small game, the wooden-tipped arrows were used. Birds were killed with an arrow fitted with four crossed sticks near the tip. It was intended merely to stun the game.

The length of the arrow was determined by measuring the distance from the tip of the second finger of the hunter, arm extended to the side, to the opposite shoulder. I believe that the arrows were generally longer than would be used by a modern archer. War arrows were made of new growth buttonwillow. This they would cut and scrape, using only the heart wood.

The making of arrow points of stone was practiced by few. I have seen hundreds of obsidian points chipped out. A piece of horn or bone was used to push, or pry, the flakes from the piece of obsidian. Sometimes blows were struck in the work, but I do not know how or why. It was only a matter of a few minutes to chip out an obsidian point.

The rear of the arrow shaft was fitted with three feathers. These were about five or six inches long. They were tied at the ends, but were left loose along the middle. Each man had a mark of his own on his arrows, so that he could prove that he had hit the game and that it had not been killed by some-one else. The mark was also of value in proving ownership of arrows recovered after being lost.

Sometimes the Indians would waterproof the sinew binding on an arrow with asphaltum that they traded from Indians who went to the west side of the valley, near where Coalinga was later located. They called such an arrow *lím-kin tú-yosh*, or "prairie falcon's arrow." Prairie falcon, the fast, white hawk, was supposed to have supernatural power, and so did most shiny, dark substances like asphaltum, as well as the black volcanic glass they made arrow points from, and the black paint the medicine men painted themselves with when they danced. This paint was mined south of Kings River. I saw Indians come from that direction to trade it with our medicine man. I also saw the medicine man prepare his paint by burning the black material in the fire. When he was through with it, it looked lots like the old stove polish we used to buy in cakes. They called the black paint *múts-ke-wik*, the same word they used for the color. The medicine man put white stripes and dots on top of this black. The white paint was ground up from crude chalk rock which they got in trade.

There were names for all of the ordinary colors in nature, but I probably do not remember all of them. *Ché-min* was the word for "blue." *Ché-min sús-suh* meant "blue eyes." *Múts-ke-wik* was the word for "black," *hah-búk-ah* for "red," *drói-ye* for "white," and *chah-cú-lu* for "yellow." They also used *hah-sín-k-he* to mean "gray," about midway between white and black.

In addition to small game, elk and deer were occasionally snared. The Choinumne also used to snare *shó-win*, the wild pigeons, from a blind on Kings River above Sycamore Creek. I have seen two Indians come in with at least a hundred pigeons apiece, snared in less than two hours. I heard one old Indian say that he alone had caught more than two hundred pigeons in one forenoon.

Snaring was done while the pigeons were watering. They liked to water at a spring or water hole near tall trees, especially pines. They seldom watered at the main river, and they all tried to water at the same hole. In the morning about an hour after sunup, they would come to water in flocks and droves, many thousands of them. They would light in such numbers that sometimes they would strip the limbs from the trees. It would take these large flights from one to three hours to water. When they left a water hole, it was as badly drained and trampled as though a thousand sheep had watered there.

Pigeon hunters built a blind close to the water hole. It was a very clever arrangement. First, a smooth platform was leveled off as close to the water as possible. Then a shallow pit was dug on the side of the platform away from the water. It was large enough to hold two men lying down. The Indians I knew often hunted in pairs. This shallow pit was covered over with a light framework of bent limbs. Brush was put on the framework so the whole thing would look like a natural growth of brush.

On the side of the brush next to the level platform was a wide opening about eighteen inches high. A curtain of grass was hung across the opening. Near the middle of the platform, and about three feet from the grass curtain, was laid a pole about six feet long and three inches in diameter. To a pigeon the whole affair was the most harmless-looking thing possible.

Each pigeon hunter had several interesting pieces of equipment. First were two long snares, called *trék-loosh*. They were made of straight elderberry branches about eight feet long. On the tip of the branch was fastened a running noose, made of twisted, springy hair. It was formed by lashing a hair string about sixteen inches long to the stick. On the loose end of the string was fastened a stiff ring about an inch in diameter. This ring was slipped back on the stick to form a "u" shaped loop, the open side of the "u" closed by the stick. The loop was about six inches in diameter.

The hunters each had a captive pigeon in a cage made of cottonwood or willow twigs. The cage was about three feet long, a foot in diameter, and pointed at each end. Each also had a large bag of netting made from milkweed fiber.

About daylight, the hunters spread some ground acorn bait on the platform and then crawled through the brush into the rear of the pit. It was dark in there, and the pigeons could not see the hunters through the grass curtain across the front.

Each hunter took out his captive pigeon and blindfolded it. Then he tied one of its legs to a stick about an inch in diameter and five or six feet long, using a piece of string a foot long. When a pigeon is blindfolded, his feet hang onto whatever they touch like two vises. The Indians stood their pigeons on the end of the stick, and then poked them out through the curtain and rested the snare on the stick lying crossways on the platform outside. The pigeon teetered on his perch and sometimes flapped his wings in order to keep his balance.

The wild pigeons came in flights that would sometimes shut out the sun like a cloud. They piled into the nearest trees until there was not a single place for another pigeon to sit. They were always wary of the water. No pigeon seemed to want to be the first to drink. In order to start them coming down, the hunters would pick up the sticks holding their decoys and move them around in the air. This made the decoys flap their wings in order to keep their balance. Immediately some of the wild pigeons decided all was safe and flew down to the platform. They saw the acorn crumbs and began eating. You understand, the pigeons were filling up on water before an all-day trip to their favorite wild rice or acorn feeding grounds, and were as hungry as they could get.

The hunters slowly slid their long snares out until a pigeon began picking up acorn meal from within the loop. The stick was then given a quick twist and a pull. The loop flipped up around the pigeon's neck and before he knew anything had happened he was flapping about and headed for the grass curtain.

By the time a pigeon had been snared, the platform was crowded with jumping, flapping, hungry pigeons, so the captured bird did not disturb the rest. Sometimes, in jerking a pigeon, two or more others would be knocked down. But they scarcely stopped eating. I have often seen two pigeons caught at the same time in one snare, and several times have seen three pulled in at once.

As soon as the hunter pulled the pigeon inside the curtain with one hand, he ran out a second loop with the other hand. He never took his eyes off the pigeons outside. He caught the captured pigeon between his knees, took off the loop, broke its neck with his thumb and forefinger, stuck it in the net, put the mouth of the net under his knee, and snaked in another pigeon with the other hand.

I helped snare pigeons twice, so I know just how it was done. It is about the only bird hunting I ever did. The old Indian I snared with could take in six or more pigeons while I was taking in one. But it was sure great sport.

We children used to snare rabbits on the plains, and sometimes squirrels and the little prairie foxes. The snares were made of bent withes and looped milkweed string.

Deer and other large game was generally dressed in the field where it was killed. The party who killed the game generally carried it in and hung it in a tree in camp. Then the women took charge of it. I never saw the women carry in a deer.

Public Life and Education

REMEMBER THAT THE CHIEF, or headman, of the tribe used to give orders about the gathering of the supply of food. He was held more or less responsible for the welfare of the whole tribe, and I believe he would have been in disgrace had he allowed the tribe to become in want. He had to settle all of the petty quarrels and differences between different members of the tribe, and still be fair and friendly to all parties concerned.

On the whole, the Indians I was with quarreled very little. An Indian can say less longer with more grace than anyone you will meet. The adult Indians very seldom ever quarreled, or even argued with each other. In general they did very little useless talking. They were not as speechless as many people suppose, but were not inclined to talk or gossip carelessly. I remember one hair pulling between two of the women, and one or two quarrels between men. The Indians I lived with were great to joke among themselves, and they all enjoyed themselves. The women were treated well by their husbands. Before they got whiskey, I never saw an Indian man strike an Indian woman.

About the method of selecting a chief, I am not sure, as I was not with them long enough to take any part in the tribal deliberations. But I am sure that if the chief, called *Té-ah*, had been lax in the performance of his duties someone else would have been selected in his stead. I do not mean that the tribe would have voted him out, but they would simply have looked to someone wise for advice and help and he would have automatically been out of his position in the tribe. Of course I may be wrong about this, but I am judging from what I saw of their life, and I believe that the headman received his leadership in the first place through the natural tendency of the members of the tribe to go to the most able member for advice.

The oldest son of the chief held a rather important position, at least in the tribe I was with. He was generally included in any deliberations, and was consulted when anything of importance was to be decided. From what I heard of their consultations I would judge that the oldest son was being prepared for, and would have succeeded to, the position of headman.

The year before I left the Indians I was about sixteen, and I remember that there was some discussion as to whether I was to be initiated into the tribe at the time when several other boys were initiated. However, it was not done, and my daddy took me from them before the time came around again the next year. In a way I have always regretted this, as I saw practically nothing of the initiation of the other boys the year before, and have always wished that I knew just what they said and did at the initiation.

At the time of the initiation ceremonies I do remember that the young boys were coached by one or two of the older men who used to tell us stories during the evenings around the fire. But I saw nothing of any sort of a ceremony.

White people generally have a wrong impression as to how the Indians bathed together in the rivers. In the first place, before sunup practically every Indian at the rancheria had taken a bath: men, women and children.

At the morning bath the men generally removed the breechcloth and bathed before the women were up. During the day, at least in summer, when they would be in the water from one to twenty times, the breechcloth was left in place and was worn while it was drying.

Young children wore no clothing at all, but I have seen many white families who thought nothing of letting their children run around without clothing.

Children were taught not to fear the water. I have seen the women take their babies down to the river when they were only a few days old. They would hold them on their open hands and dip their backs in the water. If the child was startled by the water they would talk to it and reassure it. Then they would dip it in again and again until it was not afraid to go completely under.

Sometimes when the baby was dipped under the water it would come up coughing, but the mother would talk to it and dip it in again until it lost all fear. They would then teach it to swim by holding it partly out of the water.

Many of the Indian children could swim almost as soon as they could walk. In fact, many of the children were kept strapped on the cradle so long that I believe they could swim before they could walk. Their word for "swim" is *ih-páh-ush*.

The women considered it a disgrace that I could not swim when I first went to live with them, and they soon made me learn how. They did not help me, but made me go out in the shallow water and imitate the other children until I learned how. I soon learned how to swim as well as any of them. We thought nothing of plunging into the river anyplace we wanted to cross. I never saw or heard of an accidental drowning among the Indians.

Sometimes the women would place a child in the deep water alone long before it could walk. They would bend a willow branch down to the water and allow the child to hold on to it. Then they would go on about their work, and some-times pay no attention to it for a quarter of an hour or more. I remember that once I thought I would have some fun, and when the woman was some distance away I shook the limb the child was clinging to. It never made a noise, but gave the blackest look I ever received.

Babies and small children were carried on the backs of the women, in a sort of wicker basket cradle. The basket cradle was a handy means of caring for the baby. When the babies were strapped to the baskets, the women always knew where to look for them. They kept some of the children strapped to the baskets a part of the time until they were at least two years old.

The Choinumne used three kinds of cradles for their children. The first was a light, flexible mat that could be rolled up. It was called *bé-eetch*. A large cradle was used when the child was about six or eight weeks old. It was made by bending a long withe into a "u" shape about a foot across and two feet long. It had a woven sunshade over it, and was carried on the woman's back by means of a flat strap made of wild milkweed fiber which crossed her forehead. Sometimes she placed an ornamented basket cap under the strap. This cradle was called *áhk-leetch*.

Another cradle was made of a forked stick with cross sticks tied to it. It was also carried by a fiber strap, and was called *wáh-tah-le*. The ends of these willow cross-sticks projected a couple of inches beyond each side. Then the framework was covered with woven grass or other materials, and the child was lashed to it, the hands being lashed down at the sides.

The lashing was done with a milkweed string which was looped over the projecting ends of the cross-sticks and was crossed over the child, much the same as a shoe is laced. Padding of bark and moss or soft grass was placed under the child, and a light skin, or in cold weather a rabbit skin blanket, was wrapped around it. The child was taken to the stream near camp several times a day, removed from the basket and washed.

When the child was being carried, which was most of the time, it was suspended by a sort of woven belt made of milkweed string. This belt, called *cháh-kit*, was passed under the basket and around the forehead of the woman. When the load was heavy *(míck-its nim sháw-nil)*, the woman wore a small basket over her head like a skull cap, the same as she would in carrying acorns.

The Indian doctors treated their patients by bloodletting. They would make a cut and suck out some blood. They also had another peculiar treatment. They would twist together some wormwood leaves and set them afire. With the glowing end of this firebrand, a stripe was burned along each side of the spinal column of the patient. They also did a great deal of howling over the patient. When a doctor had lost several patients, the relatives of the last deceased had the right to kill him. He was shot with arrows, or stoned to death, and made no resistance. An Indian doctor was considered *trip-nee*, which means supernatural.

In general, the young people and children were very respectful to old people. I do not remember having seen an old person slighted, or treated disrespectfully by anyone. Of course, when old people became helpless they would do nothing for them, and sometimes they suffered a great deal. I have heard white people tell about the Indians abandoning old people in order to allow them to die, and also about them being buried alive, but I never saw anything like that done.

The bodies were prepared for burial by being tied with the knees under the chin and the arms doubled at the sides. The grave was dug with pointed sticks used in digging grass nuts. The soil was carried out in baskets. Anyone except the close relations helped to dig the grave.

The mourning generally went on for several days. They would stand around the grave as it was being filled and cry and moan. Sometimes they would keep this up day and night. The mother, or wife of the deceased, was the only one to cut her hair and use the pitch and charcoal.

Trip to Tulare Lake

FTER I HAD BEEN with the Indians periodically for several months the time came for them to make one of their annual pilgrimages to Tulare Lake, which they called *Pah-áh-su*. I am sure that it was their habit to go there yearly. The lake shore was held by the Tache tribe, but the tribe I was with was quite friendly with the Taches, and they made no objection to our using the lake shore.

A great, long tule raft, called *áh-ya*, was built. They used to build small tule rafts that would carry one or two persons for use on Kings River below the rancheria opposite Sycamore Creek, but this raft for the lake trip was at least fifty feet long. It was made up of three long bundles of tules, pointed at each end, and bound together with willow withes.

The three bundles were made separately and then bound, or lashed, together with one at the bottom and two above, making a sort of keeled boat with a depression along the center of the deck. The tules were lashed together in such a way that the raft was pointed at the ends and resembled a great cigar, except that the pointed ends were turned up so that they were two or three feet above the deck.

Along the center of this raft was piled their dunnage. This dunnage consisted of supplies and camp equipment, and included mortars and pestles, baskets of acorns, acorn bread, seeds, meat, skins for bedding and many other things. On the sides of the boat sat eight or ten Indians, generally one or two families.

This raft that we used was not built to exclude water like a boat does. Tules will float on the water, and the Indians made use of their buoyancy. On the lake, and sometimes in sloughs along the river, the tules used to float about loose. The wind would drift them into great mats near the shore. The fish used to collect under these mats and we used to walk over them and spear fish from them. I believe the Indians got their idea for the rafts from these great mats of floating tules. I remember that once we bundled some of these floating tules together and used them as a boat.

For us children, the trip to Tulare Lake was an occasion of great excitement. We were all eyes and ears and could scarcely contain ourselves.

The trip was made in the late spring when the flood from the melting snows in the mountains provided enough water in the river to float the raft over the sandbars.

The whole rancheria did not make the trip. As I recollect, three rafts were built the first year. They were built several miles below Sycamore Creek, just how far I cannot say. We were almost a day carrying dunnage from Sycamore down to the place where the rafts were built. It could have been ten miles below the rancheria. I do remember that the river was wide there, and that great quantities of tules grew in a slough leading out from the river. It was in this slough that the raft had been built.

When we were all aboard, the boats were poled out into the stream and allowed to drift with the current. Three or four of the men stood at the sides of the raft and kept it away from snags and in the main current. In this way we floated along at about two or three miles an hour.

At night the raft was moored to the bank in a quiet place and we camped on the shore. It was really one of the greatest experiences I have ever had, and certainly the greatest I had while living with the Indians. I believe that they, too, enjoyed these trips more than any of their other experiences. We traveled in style and in comfort. The river was lined with trees and wild blackberry and grape vines, and the whole trip was one beautiful scene after another. In after years I used to cross Kings River many times on the bridge south of Kingsburg, and the scene there always reminded me of our trips.

Of the amount of time used in making the trip to the lake shore I have no accurate recollection. We traveled very slowly and hunted a great deal along the way. Sometimes the hunters did not board the boat at all during the day, but met us with game when we had made camp in the evening. I suppose that it must have taken us at least ten days to go from Sycamore Creek to Tulare Lake.

Occasionally we met or saw Indians from other tribes along the river. They were all friendly and seemed to take our trip as a matter of course. I remember that once a party of three of these Indians rode with us all day.

At the lake we made a permanent camp on some high ground along a slough. I believe that they had used this place before, as one of the women dug up a mortar and pestle that had been buried there previously.

We found the lake Indians near us living in some ways quite differently from the Indians at Sycamore Creek. They talked enough of our language that we could understand them readily, but the rest of their life differed more than the language.

The houses at the lake were the thing I noticed most. I do not remember having seen a house there like those upstream. Generally they were built of thin tule mats and were quite long—some of them were at least one hundred feet long. A sort of wooden ridge was erected on crotched poles set in the ground, and the tule mats were leaned up against it. Everything else was of a more temporary nature than I was used to at Sycamore Creek.

The shore lines of Tulare Lake changed and shifted a great deal. If a strong wind came from the north, as it often did, the water would move several miles south, and would move again when the wind changed. Then, when the water level in the lake changed, both the lea and windward shorelines shifted long distances. At some point it was possible to wade out into the lake as far as a mile and find the water below our knees. This made it impossible for the Indians to stay in one place permanently and they could roll up their light houses and load them on tule rafts and move in a few hours.

While we were at the lake I noticed one or two houses that have ever since been more or less of a puzzle to me. They were built in the standing tules, and seemed to be woven from the living tules as they stood in place. They were dome-shaped and about ten feet in diameter. I never saw any more of them and I have never since met anyone who had seen one of them. As I remember them, the tules appeared to have been cut away inside the house, but no excavation had been made as was made for the willow houses upstream.

The tule mats that I have mentioned were called *páh-tuk tríhnee*. They were made in two ways. Some were tied together with tule by a series of half hitches. The tules were laid out on the ground parallel to each other and close together. Then about every foot or so they were tied together by cross tules and the half hitches.

Other mats were laid out in the same way, and a milkweed string was passed through them. Holes were punched in the tules by means of a bone awl, and the string was run through the holes. These mats were used for floor coverings and mattresses, as I have mentioned, and for many other purposes. At the lake a light framework of driftwood was set up and the tule mats laid over it to provide a shade. This shade was used in other places, but was generally covered with brush instead of tule mats. It was called *chíh-mil*.

The milkweed string, called *chíh-tik*, was made of a tall milkweed that grew on the plains and foothills. It was a velvety, bluish-green weed, consisting principally of a straight stalk from three to four feet in height. Along the stalk were leaves, and at the top was a blossom which later developed into seed pods.

On the outside of the woody center was a covering of fiber considerably like flax. During the winter this loose fiber was gathered after it had fallen from the dead stalks to the ground and was used in making string. The string was twisted by means of a small stick rolled on the thigh.

When twisted, the string had much the appearance of the common sack twine used for sewing grain bags. The milkweed string was used for an almost unlimited number of purposes.

The Indians who lived on the river below Centerville also made string from the fiber of a kind of wild hemp, a tall, straight-stalked plant with red bark. They pounded the stalks between two rocks and removed the fiber with their fingers. It made a red string and was as strong as that made from milkweed.

From the sap of the same milkweed used for making the string a sort of chewing gum was made. This was obtained in a rather peculiar way. The green milkweed stalk was cut. The milk immediately began to form in a large drop on the cut end. This end was dabbed on a clay ball. This was repeated as often as a drop of milk would form on the cut end. Then another cut was made, and the process was repeated. The milk dried on the clay ball in a sort of gummy coating. This coating was peeled off and chewed. It was about the same as ordinary chewing gum after the sugar has been dissolved from it in chewing.

For fishing and hunting on the lake, a tule raft was used. This raft was constructed in a different way from the one I have already described. It was wide and flat and would pass over very shallow water. It was pointed at the ends, but the points were not raised as high as they were on the raft used on the river.

In the center of the fishing raft was a large hole. Through this hole fish were gigged much as they were from the platform on the river. The fisherman lay on his stomach with his head and shoulders over this hole, which was covered with a tule mat so he could see into the water without being seen by the fish.

A few feet ahead of the hole was an earthen, or mud, hearth. On this hearth a fire was kindled, and the cooking was done.

Sometimes three or four Indians would go out on the lake on one of the fishing rafts and hunt ducks and geese and stay out there as long as a week. During this time they poled the raft around through the tules and ate and slept on it.

They would throw loose tules over the raft and themselves, forming a blind. Then, through the hole in the center they would slowly pole the raft wherever they wanted to go. In this way they would approach within a few feet of ducks and geese and shoot them from the blind with bows and arrows.

Sometimes they would catch the ducks that flew overhead in a net. This net was a good deal like the net fishermen use to take trout out of the water after they have hooked them. It was about two feet across at the mouth. They also snared ducks and geese among the tules.

The Indians could imitate the call of almost any animal or bird, and they used to make use of this in hunting. They commonly called ducks, geese, rabbits and deer.

The tribe I was with had an interesting way of catching fish on the lake shore. A weir of willow wickerwork was built out at an angle from the shore for a distance of fifty or sixty yards. Then a large group of Indians would wade out beyond the weir. This group would form a semicircle sometimes a mile long.

After the circle was completed they would close in, all splashing and yelling and driving the fish into the shallow water behind the weir. In this shallow water were two or three Indians wading about, each with one of the bottomless wicker baskets that they used up the river for catching fish in pools.

When they felt a fish with their feet or saw a ripple made by a fish, they would clap the basket down and catch it. It was not possible to see the fish as the shallow water soon became very muddy.

One of the great sports at the lake was the jackrabbit drive. The flat sagebrush plains around the lake were fairly alive with jackrabbits, and the Indians used to plan a drive much like the drives later made by the white people, except that they used no pen or corral.

A milkweed string net was made. This was about thirty feet long and four feet high. It was tied just like an ordinary fish seine, but I never saw the Indians seine fish. This net was used only for catching rabbits. The net was erected between two large sage bushes. Then a long line of Indians marched out at an angle from each end of it. Most of these Indians carried a stick about two feet long. When the two lines of Indians had formed wings several hundred yards long the outer ends closed in and then they drove the enclosed rabbits toward the net.

When an Indian came close enough to a rabbit he would throw his stick spinning at it and would generally break its legs. But most of the rabbits were killed at the net.

As the rabbits ran along between the two lines of Indians they saw what they thought was an opening in the line at the net. They attempted to run through this opening, but hit the net and bounced back. Then they were promptly clubbed by one of two or three Indians who were hiding there for that purpose.

It surely was exciting when the drivers had closed in. There would be hundreds of rabbits and almost as many sticks flying in the air. Many of the rabbits would break through the line of Indians and escape, but a great many, probably two hundred, would be killed in a forenoon drive.

The rabbit skins were made into fine blankets, which

the Choinumnes called *chih-cú-nah*. These were used as a covering for sleeping much as an ordinary blanket. They were the warmest and most comfortable bed covering I have ever used.

The skins were taken from the rabbits without being split, and while green they were cut into long strips about three-quarters of an inch wide. As the strips dried, they naturally curled up with the flesh side inside and the fur on the outside. This made a sort of fur boa about an inch and a half in diameter.

In making the blanket, two of the strings were twisted together for a distance of about six feet. Then the ends were doubled back and looped through the twists of the first portion. Working back and forth across the blanket in this way it was woven into a square about six feet on each side.

Smaller blankets were used as a sort of cape, or shawl, in extremely cold weather, or to wrap the babies in before they were strapped on the cradle. The women also made their skirts in this way.

We used to see elk and antelope around the lake. I heard about the Indians surrounding antelope, but I never saw it done. They used to shoot both elk and antelope from blinds when they came to the lake to water.

Antelope were easily killed with arrows, but elk were almost too much for them. It was almost impossible for them to kill an elk outright with their weapons. They would shoot arrows into an elk and then follow it for several days until it was weak enough to be overpowered.

My brother, Ben, once killed an elk on Tulare Lake. When he was dressing it, he noticed an unnatural growth inside the body. Upon investigating, he found it to be the foreshaft of an arrow which had lodged there and had entirely healed over, both inside and outside.

Indian and Anglo Conflicts Begin

MADE TWO TRIPS to Tulare Lake with the Indians. If my memory is accurate, they were made in the summers of 1853 and 1854. I do not believe that my tribe made any such excursions later than 1855, as the reservations had broken up their routine. They had been deprived of their game and were rapidly starved and crowded into the hills in competition with their hostile mountain neighbors. I never saw one of the large tule rafts after the second trip.

One thing happened on our second trip to the lake that I will never forget. I had not seen my daddy for a year or more. He had been away with horses and cattle and hogs, in the mountains and on the plains, and I did not know where he was.

It was late in the forenoon of a hot, sultry, summer day. Several Indian boys and I were shooting with our bows and arrows at a dummy duck in the edge of the lake. We used to do this almost every day, and sometimes we would be lucky enough to get a shot at a fish. I saw a party of three horsemen passing at a distance of several hundred yards.

I watched the travelers until they passed us. Something about them was puzzling to me, and I finally saw that one of them was my daddy. I will never forget how lost and helpless I felt at the time. My heart seemed to sink down to my feet. I wanted to see him so badly, and I was sure I could not catch him. But I ran after him anyway, and called to him, hoping to attract his attention.

Of course he neither heard nor saw me. However, I kept on until I could go no farther and, after falling down several times and becoming hot and entirely out of breath and helpless, I lay in the tules, crying.

One of the Indians who was fishing about a quarter of a mile or more away, closer to where my daddy was passing, saw what was going on. He ran out from the lake and stopped them. Then they rode back to where I was. I was still lying in the tules, because I was ashamed to let the Indian boys see that I was crying, and was feeling about as homesick as I have ever felt. I did not know what had been done after I had fallen, and was about as surprised a boy as ever lived when my daddy rode up and took me on his horse.

My daddy had not expected to see me at the lake. He had left us at Sycamore Creek. But the Indians had made a trip to the lake in the meantime, and he had not known of it.

After my daddy took me on his horse, the Indians, who had been fishing nearby, collected about and led him to their camp. He stayed with us about an hour and had dinner. Then he had to go to look after some cattle he was rounding up, and I did not see him again for about two years.

All of the Indians, even the children, were very serious about this experience of mine and never teased me, or made any reference to my crying, as I know they would have under any other circumstances. They were afraid that my daddy would take me away with him and were pleased when he left me. I was willing to stay with the Indians and did not ask him to take me with him.

At the time of our second trip to the lake, one other thing happened that I will never forget. The government had been trying to establish Indian reservations on Kings and Fresno Rivers and a troop of cavalry was attempting to round up all of the Indians in the valley. The Indians had been dying off rapidly in the few years previous to the establishment of the reservations and there were not many of them left. But even with the few Indians, it was almost impossible, as the Indians did not want to go on the reservation. I never blamed them for this, as it was simply a means of getting their land away from them and they knew it. They scattered and hid in the tules. All of our group at the lake escaped.

There was a white man by the name of Mann living near the lake with his Indian wife. They had been living there for several years. A squad of cavalry rode up to the door of the cabin one day and demanded the woman. Mann told them that she was his wife; that he had provided for her for several years, and that he could continue to do so in the future.

The leader of the squad told Mann to bring her out, and when Mann refused he knocked the door open and entered the cabin. The woman had crawled under the bed, and the cavalrymen started to drag her out. She called to Mann for help. Mann ran to her aid and was shot in the back and killed by one of the troopers outside.

The troopers tied the woman and took her with them and left Mann lying where he had fallen. The Indians I was with knew Mann and buried him after the squad of cavalry left. I did not see what happened, but some of the Indians of our party did. A short time afterward, we saw the woman who had been taken away when Mann was killed. I have many times heard her tell what happened.

I expect that this story about the killing of Mann sounds pretty bad and probably a number of other things I am telling about the Indians and the white people may give the impression that I favor the Indians and am prejudiced against the white people. In the first place, I have never talked about my life with the Indians because I had very little to tell that the white people liked to hear. I knew the Indians in their natural state and I know that they were the finest people that I have ever met. I am not telling what I would like to be able to tell; only what I heard and saw.

Indian Morals

THERE IS NO USE trying to deny that the Indians I knew were, for the most part, naked savages. But I have found in the sixty-six or more years since I left them that just wearing a lot of clothes does not make people decent. Neither does going around naked necessarily make people indecent.

There was nothing in the Indian language that compared with our profanity and vulgarity. They did not have the indecent attitude that white people have. They had no cash registers or padlocks. Everything they possessed was left in the open and was safe from being stolen or being molested in any way.

The Indians, even the children, were very modest in their ideas about their own abilities. But I remember one exception. A boy about fifteen years of age was called *Búh-sho,* which meant "braggart." Another was named *Múh-loosh,* which meant "cheat." Another Indian boy was very nosy for an Indian. He was always watching anything that was going on. His name was *Bo-có-lah,* meaning "snooper."

I seldom ever knew the Indians to cheat at anything. I remember that when we played their game of water tag, some of the Indian boys would swim deep into the muddy water and I would have to go down after them. As soon as I touched one of them, he would immediately come up and take my place. I did not know whom I had tagged, but there was never any argument. And when I was down I never had one claim he had touched me when he had not. I never remember hearing an argument of any kind in an Indian game. I remember that when I started to school near Venice Hill with the white boys in 1862 I was surprised to find I could not trust them to tell the truth when we played water tag. So I quit playing it with them.

The Indians had their own ideas of proper manners. It was very bad manners to be impolite to old people. In fact, children were almost never impolite to old people. When an Indian woman had something choice to give to the children, probably sugar-pine sugar or candy she had traded for at Centerville, she would say, *"Joul-bú-sho,"* which meant "I have something to divide up." All the children within hearing would come on the run. But they would not crowd each other. They would wait their turn. And each got an equal share. If one put himself before the others, the Indian woman would say, *"Ta-míd-um,"* meaning "Where are your manners?" The child would be so embarrassed he would refuse his portion and would go and hide. If a child upset a basket of acorn mush or got into something he shouldn't, which was very seldom, his mother would say, *"To-trá-shee-uh."* *To-tree* meant bad; so she said, "That is bad business."

The average Indian I knew was more reliable than the average white man I knew in after years. They knew how to make fermented liquor, because their sweet manzanita wine would ferment when they kept it too long. But it was thrown out when it fermented. I never knew an Indian to make any sort of fermented liquor to drink. The first person who ever offered me a drink of fermented liquor was a white man.

The Indians knew the use of tobacco, but they used it sparingly. I do not believe that an Indian naturally smoked more than one or two puffs in three or four days.

They also knew the use of a strong narcotic, the tea from the root of the Jimson weed. But it was used only once in a lifetime, when the young man was being initiated into the tribe. I never saw or heard of an Indian using a native narcotic habitually.

The moral conditions in the Indian rancheria where I stayed were better than they were in the white villages that grew up nearby. They were better there in the sixties than they were in any of the rest of the towns I knew in those days, or since. I do not mean that everyone in the white towns was bad, but that a great many things went on there that were unheard of at the rancheria.

[There were three people who lived in two houses about 300 yards away from any of the other houses.] I paid no attention to these people until after I had been with the Indians for maybe eight years. I had supposed that all three were women. But I saw that one of them was a man. He was dressed just like the women. He never came into the village among the other Indians. He lived alone. I never saw anyone go into his house, but I was told by the older boys that some of the men did go to his house after nightfall.

Before I left the Indians I talked with some of the older Indians, both men and women, about this man. They told me that he was not allowed to associate with the people in the village, that he was not like the other men. He went on seed-gathering and other gathering trips with the two other women and helped them pound acorns and prepare their foods. He had a bow and arrows and a stuffed deer's head of his own and killed deer for himself and the two women. I remember that the Indians in the village called him *Hah-wah-chah*. I do not know whether that was his real name or whether that was the name for a person like him.

The two women in the other house were not allowed to go into the village either. The rest of the Indians called them by a bad name, which I have forgotten. Later I learned that white people call such people prostitutes. I never saw anyone else go into this house either, but the older boys told me that some of the men went there after dark. I remember that the men would not talk to me about these two women. So I asked the Indian woman who was keeping me about them. She told me that they were bad women and that some of the men went to the house and stayed until before daylight, that she had watched the place all night several times and had seen the men go in and come out.

The girls were not promiscuous. I only heard of two girls who were said to be so and everybody called them by the names for prostitutes.

Yet, the reason that my daddy left me with the Indians until I was about seventeen, instead of taking me from them when I was old enough to take care of myself, was because he said that I was in better company with the Indians than I would be staying around the white towns with him. There I would be in contact with saloons, gamblers, drunks, bums and many other undesirables that I would not know at the rancheria.

Many of the white settlers of the sixties will disagree with me about many of the things I am mentioning. But they could not, and never did, know those Indians in their natural state.

Crowded Out by Settlers

FTER THE RESERVATION was formed and the white settlers began to come into the valley in great numbers,
the Indians had a hard time of it. I used to hear all of
their troubles discussed at the rancheria where I lived, and I
know how they felt about the way they were treated.

The elk and antelope were all gone in just a few years.
Fences were built and the Indians were not allowed to roam
about and gather plants and seeds and hunt as they had done
before. They were forced into contact with the Monaches and
other mountain Indians. I believe that this had as much to do
with their disappearance as anything else.

They were finally crowded into small camps and had to
shear sheep and wash clothes for the white settlers about
them. White men were always furnishing them liquor and many
of them were killed by whiskey. Whiskey made devils of them.
Quarrels and fights would take place between parties who had
always been friends and when such quarrels arose, someone
was sure to be badly knifed or shot. The older men of the tribe
tried to stop them, but could do nothing with them.

The Indians were quite honest among themselves and never
stole from one another. I believe they were more truthful among
themselves than the white people. The early settlers used to
be scandalized when a white man married an Indian woman. I
believe that in nine cases out of ten the woman was the loser
in the bargain and was better than the man she married.

The Indians realized that the white people were smarter
and cleverer than they were and they looked to the whites
many times for advice until they found they could not trust
them at all. They would do many things when advised to by

the whites that they would not think of doing upon the advice of their own people. In their own life marriage consisted simply of providing a home for the bride. Many white scamps would fix up a cabin for one of the Indian women and then when they wanted to would go away and leave her. She would provide for and raise the children. Many times she was better off when he did leave, as she otherwise had to provide for him also.

Then, too, some of the Indians started living in houses. They could not stand an indoor life and many died of consumption and measles. When they had these diseases, they would go in the sweat house and sweat for an hour or more and then jump in the cold streams. This killed them by the hundreds.

They had never known about fevers. The sweat house was a good remedy for rheumatism, but it was deadly when used as a treatment for fevers.

When I left the Indians for the last time in 1862, there were not more than forty left, of a group that numbered more than three hundred when I went to them in 1850 or 1851. Battles with the whites accounted for very few of those missing, for the Indians I was with, as a group, had no battles with the whites. I believe that a few of the young men joined in some of the difficulties for the excitement they could get from it, but only a very few individuals.

Return from Tulare Lake—
Life Resumes

E LEFT THE LAKE for the last time in the summer. We were all sorry to go. There was an almost unlimited amount of game there and always lots of excitement in hunting and fishing. The lake was a great attraction to the Indians, just as it later was to the white people.

Of the trip upstream, I remember very little. We started back with our supplies piled on the raft and poled it as far up the river as the slack water extended. Then the women loaded the dunnage on their backs and we trudged back to Sycamore Creek. The rafts were abandoned at the side of the river.

I am sure that we carried back none of the portable stone mortars and pestles that we had rafted down earlier in the summer. It is my belief that they were buried at the lake camp site for future use. Although I saw nothing like that done, I believe I have mentioned that when we arrived at the lake, one of the women dug up a mortar that she had buried there previously.

It probably took us longer to make the trip from the lake back to Sycamore Creek than it had taken to make the down trip. I kept no record of the time, but I remember that it was a long, hot journey and that we were weary when we arrived back at the rancheria.

Following our arrival back at the rancheria, I was with the Indians almost continually until about 1857. After that I was with them most of the time, but I stayed with my daddy and my brothers when they were at home.

During this time I hunted and fished with the Indians and learned all about their way of living. By this time, the Indians were wearing old cast-off clothing, given to them by the white people. I dressed like my brothers, wearing the common work clothes of the day.

Many people do not know how the breechcloth and gee string were made and used. A strip about ten inches wide was cut out of the middle of a deer skin, using the longest portion, from the neck to the tail. This strip was called by the white people a "breech clout," but the Indians had a name of their own for it which I have forgotten *[háw-awk]*. The gee string was a narrow string of buckskin long enough to pass around the waist and tie. They called it *chíh-tik*.

The breechcloth was folded across the middle of the gee string much as a towel would be folded across a clothesline. It was then placed behind the wearer, and the ends of the gee string brought around to the front. The ends of the breech-cloth were brought between the legs to the front and held against the heart, under the chin. The ends of the gee string were tied over the front of the breechcloth. Then the ends of the breechcloth were allowed to drop down and hang loose in front, like a small apron.

This completed the wearing apparel of the men except in cold weather, when a mountain lion skin might be tied about the shoulders. They wore no foot covering of any sort and had no word in their language for anything of the kind. Their feet were as tough as any shoe.

The women wore a rabbit skirt woven together like the blanket. They called it *chú-moosh*. This was made of two aprons, one in front and one behind. The apron behind was smaller than that in front. These aprons reached about to the knees of the wearers.

Both men and women wore their hair long. I do not believe that it was customary for them to braid their hair in the days before they came in contact with the white people. I never saw one of the real old Indians with braided hair. Neither did the

Indians naturally shake hands. They hugged each other about the shoulders like Frenchmen, an act they called *cáw-bush*.

The women cut their hair off in front in bangs, which they called *dil-wú-shuh*, but the men left their hair long across the front. Both men and women sometimes smeared their hair with bear oil. This made it shine much as is stylish among the young white fellows today.

Although I never saw a bald-headed Indian in my life, they had a word in their language that exactly fit a bald head. It was *tahl-sís-in*. They used this word in referring to a bare piece of ground or a bare hilltop, and they were not slow to apply it to white people when they saw a bald-headed one.

The men kept their hair out of their eyes by tying a string around the head just above the eyes, the hair having been parted and thrown back over the shoulders. The string tied around the head was made of milkweed fiber and had twisted into it down from the breast of the eagle. It looked, when new, like a small feather boa about an inch in diameter. After it had been worn a while it became more compact, a little larger than a lead pencil. The down string was wound around the head three or four times and then tied. Inside of it and into the hair at the back of the head were stuck several feathers. Some of these feathers were left in their natural state, and some were dyed pretty colors.

There was something of importance about the down from the breast of the eagle, but I am not sure of its significance. I do know that they held the eagle in a good deal of awe, and that only certain persons were allowed to kill them.

The Indians would never drink from a spring or stream if there were small feathers or down near it. I remember having asked some of the Indians about this. They told me such places were poison. I do not believe that this was the real reason, but that they just did not want me to drink from such places.

I know that the medicine man, or Indian doctor, used to

keep a small bag of down and that in some of his doctoring he used to scatter some of it before the wind. I suppose that when an Indian came to a spring with down around it he thought the medicine man had been making some sort of magic there.

The Indians had little or no beard. The young men pulled it out with a sort of tweezers made of a split stick until it did not grow in again to any great extent. Some of the men allowed their moustaches to grow. They called a moustache *dáh-mut*.

The tweezers that the Indians used to pull their whiskers out with were called *go-gó-ish*. Their beards they called *táh-muh*. While I was with them, they got a white man's razor, and some of them shaved with it. They called this *kaht-táoo-shish*. I never thought to ask them whether they had shaved in the old days. They may have done it when I saw them simply for the novelty of it. But they must have done something of the kind before, or they would not have had a word for it. Of course, in the old days, they would have had nothing better than a sharp piece of rock to shave with. The word for "short" was *áh-tutch*. When they wanted anything shortened they said, *"ah-tútch-lah."* Neither this word nor any other I ever heard had any relation to the word they used for shaving.

A very good brush was made of the husk of the tall soaproot. It was used to brush the hair. It had curved bristles. The Indians called it *trö-kote*. Another such brush was made with straight bristles and was used for brushing the acorn flour out of the mortars. One end of the husk was tied with milkweed string to make the brush. Then the mashed pulp of the bulb about which the husk had grown was placed over the handle. This dried and kept the fiber of the husk from loosening and falling out. This same pulp was used to waterproof and sunproof the cover for the baby cradle by means of which the babies were carried on the backs of the women.

A common article about an Indian house was a dried goose

or duck wing. It was dried partly spread open and was used as a brush. It made a very good one too. I rememer that the Indians gave Mother one. She used it to brush crumbs off the table.

The paint used by the Indians I knew was red and white. They would paint their faces red and then paint white stripes across them. As a sign of mourning, the women used to cover their faces and hair with a mixture of pine pitch and charcoal. Some of the near relatives also cut their hair short as a sign of mourning.

The women used to tattoo their chins. They would make cuts on their chins with small, sharp chips of rock and rub charcoal into the cuts. I do not know of any reason for the painting or tattooing except that I believe the men used to paint up for special occasions.

Both men and women wore beads around their necks. Some of the women pierced their noses, which they called *trúh-luk cáh-new*. After piercing it, a woman would run a slim piece of shell or bone through her nose. This piece of bone would be five or six inches long, and was called *cha*. Most of them pierced their ears and wore shells in them.

Conflict and Tragedy

NOT LONG AFTER I returned from the second trip to the lake [I went to stay for a while with my daddy, and we] began having trouble with the Monache Indians from across the mountains. They used to hang around and steal corn and anything else they could find. The local Indians used to keep a watch for us and notify us when they saw anything stolen. Matters got worse and worse until we had quite a war with them.

The beginning of the trouble was with an Indian who had stolen some corn. The friendly Indians told us who it was who stole the corn. My daddy watched for the thief and finally had an opportunity to catch him. He tied the thief to a tree. His companions stood around and watched to see what was going to happen. They made no move to rescue their tribesman, but when they saw what my daddy was going to do, they became very much excited and called to me to turn the Indian loose.

My daddy could understand the Indians almost as well as I could, and he told me to "let that Indian alone until I have finished with him."

He cut the Indian's hair off close up to his head. The Indian howled and struggled worse than if his head was being cut off. In fact, if he had known that his head was going to be cut off I am sure he would never have made a sound. Nor would his companions have said anything. It was a terrible disgrace for an Indian to have his hair cut off. It either meant that he had been caught stealing, or that he was in mourning.

After this experience matters grew worse all the time. We had to keep our weapons with us all of the time and we saw the Monaches sneaking about day and night.

I had been giving the Indians sugar and coffee and other things they liked when they would come to the house and beg for it. My daddy told me not to do it any more.

One day my daddy was working quite a distance up the creek. He had told Ben to do some work at the house, but Ben had stopped work and was spearing trout in a water hole near the house. He had a couple of trout lying on the bank of the stream. One of the Monache Indians came to me and told me that my daddy had said that he could have the fish. I was sure that such was not the case, as my daddy did not know that Ben was fishing. In fact, he had told Ben not to fish, but to keep at work.

I told the Indian he would have to wait until my daddy came and gave him the fish. This made the Indian angry, as he could see that I knew he was not telling the truth. He stood there a few minutes and then asked for a drink of water. I gave him a dipper of water, but kept my eyes on him, as I knew he was up to some mischief; if he had really wanted a drink of water, he would have gone to the creek instead of asking me.

The Indian took a drink and then filled his mouth with water. He started letting the water run out in his hands like he was going to wash them. When he had filled his hands he quickly threw it all in my face. I grabbed my bow and arrows, which were nearby, and he started to run.

When he had gone about thirty yards he had to jump a ditch. Just as he jumped the ditch, I hit him in the back with an arrow. It must have penetrated several inches, but he kept on running and reached back and pulled the arrow out.

He ran to where Ben was fishing and told him what I had done, showing him the arrow. Then he went up the creek on the run. Ben knew that my daddy was up there alone and that there were more of the Monaches around there and he felt sure there would be trouble. So he ran down to where I was and asked me what the trouble was. I told him what had happened. Then he said, "Don't you know it's bad business to shoot an Indian?" "Yes," I said, "but it's bad business for an Indian to throw water in my face, too."

About this time I came down with chills and fever. I was lying in bed and Ben was at the back of the house making a rawhide hackamore. From where I lay, I could look out of the door, and I saw six or eight Indians coming up the trail. They stopped and squatted down under a big oak tree where we used to keep game hanging. They were Monaches and had their bows and arrows with them. They were in paint, and, as they had no women or children with them, I was sure they were bent on mischief.

One of the Monaches I knew came in where I was. He sat down close to me and asked me how I was. I told him that I was getting better. When he was close enough he grabbed me by the throat and started choking me. I threw my knee up and knocked him far enough away that I was able to yell.

When I yelled Ben ran in. None of them had seen Ben until then. He grabbed a chair we had made of willows and rawhide and hit the Indian over the head with it. The Indian fell down and Ben started striking him over the shoulders and back with the chair.

By this time I could see that the other Indians were stringing their bows and I called to Ben, telling him about it. He dropped the chair, gave the Indian a kick, grabbed his rifle in one hand and me under the other arm, and ran out the back door. He wanted to get behind the stone chimney, as they could drive their arrows through the oak shakes on the side of the house.

Ben laid me down behind the chimney and then tried to get a shot at the Indians. By this time they had changed their minds about making trouble, and were making tracks instead. They were so far away and were running so fast that Ben did not shoot.

A few days after the Indian choked me, Ben and a man by the name of William Campbell were working in the corn some distance above the house. Suddenly the arrows began to fly, and Campbell was hit in the thigh by one of them. He fell down and Ben grabbed his rifle, which he always kept within a few feet of him.

The Indians kept shooting and so did Ben. From where Campbell was lying on the ground he could see the legs of an Indian a few yards behind Ben. He called Ben. Ben turned around just as the Indian bobbed up from behind a rock and snapped an arrow at him. Ben saw the arrow just in time to turn sideways and draw in his stomach quickly. The arrow just grazed his shirt front. The next time the Indian bobbed up to shoot, Ben shot him between the eyes. After the rest of the Indians had cleared out, Campbell and Ben went over to look at the Indian who had been shot. He was the same Indian I had shot in the back with an arrow.

By this time it was not safe to stay in the canyon, so they took me down to the ranch of John A. Patterson. This, as I remember, was about ten miles below Sycamore Creek. I believe Patterson lived about three miles above Centerville. That evening when the vaqueros came in, they told of having trouble with the Indians. One saddle horse had been shot in the neck and another in the hip, by arrows. One of the vaqueros had an arrow through his clothes.

At the Patterson ranch and in the vicinity, they mustered about thirty or forty men and went back and ran the Indians out of the country. I do not know how many they killed and do not believe they did either, but they claimed thirty.

When we left the house at Sycamore Creek before the battle with the Monaches, we had closed it up. When we came back after the battle we found that nothing had been disturbed. Our friends at the rancheria had kept a guard over it and had not allowed the Monaches to molest anything.

When we first went to Kings River the Indians had no guns. A few years later some of them had guns and they used to come to our place and beg for caps and powder. My daddy would never let them have any. In the battle on Sycamore Creek they had nothing but bows and arrows.

In the early days on the San Joaquin and Kings Rivers we used the bow and arrow and fish gig as much as possible because the noise of our guns would discover us to the Monaches. This was one of the reasons we were glad to get the fresh game from the valley Indians. While the Monaches would not have made an open attack upon us during the early part of our stay at Sycamore Creek, if they had caught one of us out alone at some distance from the house, they might have done away with him.

At the beginning of our trouble, when I had come in the house after shooting the Monache in the back with an arrow, I had set the bow and the five remaining arrows in the corner of the cabin. I did not think about them for some time, and when I went to get them they were gone. No one seemed to know where they were. One evening we were sitting on the porch and I said to Ben, "What do you suppose ever came of my bow and arrows?" Then he told me that my daddy had thrown them in the creek the same evening I had shot the Indian. He was afraid I would cause some more trouble. It was the best bow I ever owned and I wish I had it now.

After the trouble with the Indians, my daddy started running hogs on Tulare Lake. My Daddy and Jack Gordon were in partnership. They took three Indians with them and went to San Luis Obispo. There they bought eight hundred head of white hogs. For just a few dollars they also bought a band of mustang horses. They drove the horses ahead of the hogs. When the hogs became hungry they would shoot one of the horses and cut it open for the hogs. The hogs would pick the bones as clean as though wolves had been eating the horse.

In this way, the hogs were kept in good shape all the way to Tulare Lake. My daddy was a great man for action. He always traveled light. He would start out on a trip over the San Joaquin plains without so much as a pack animal. He would put some bread and jerky in a sack, roll it up in a blanket, tie the blanket behind the saddle, fill a couple of large canteens with water and he was ready for a three weeks' trip.

My daddy and Gordon put their hogs on Tulare Lake to feed on tule roots and mussels. After the hogs had fattened at the lake, they were taken to the Sierra foothills. At that time of the year the acorns were ripe and they drove the hogs north through the acorn belt and sold them at the mines in Mariposa and Tuolumne counties. This venture proved to be quite profitable.

Jack Gordon was a bandit. The hog business was merely a cover under which he carried on many depredations. My daddy suspected this for a long time and after he was sure about Gordon's activities outside of the hog business he found some excuse for dissolving the partnership. Gordon was clever in his dealings and was not generally suspected of any crooked work. Mike Mitchell's father and my daddy were about the only persons who really knew his real character. Gordon was a dangerous man and would shoot to kill upon the slightest provocation. He was later connected with the Mason-Henry gang.

By 1860 my daddy began staying around Visalia most of the time. He had taken up a piece of land near there and kept several good horses that he entered in the races at the track in Visalia.

When the Civil War broke out, conditions were bad in the Four Creeks country. Almost everyone around there was a southerner and they had to establish a military post, called Camp Babbitt, to keep them in order—to keep Visalia from seceding from the Union, as some of the southerners around there used to say. My daddy was a southerner and his sympathies were with the

South. But when it came to actually taking up arms against the Union, he could not do it. I guess he had been in the army too much to change to the Confederate army.

About this time, my daddy decided that I had been with the Indians long enough. So early in 1862, he took me over to Visalia and put me in school. When I started to school, I believe that my speech must have been a little peculiar from having talked so much Indian. It may have been that I unconsciously used a few Indian words. At least the boys at school used to make fun of me. I had to whip every boy in school before they would let me alone about it.

Then, too, there seemed at this time in the minds of many white people to be some sort of a stigma attached to my life with the Indians. Whether they thought I was some sort of squaw man or half breed I do not know. I had considerable trouble over this while I was around Visalia and had to whip several persons because of it.

From then on I resolved to never speak of my life with the Indians. People in general had so many wrong notions about Indians and were so ignorant about their lives that I was continually drawn into arguments about them. Everyone was so sure they knew all about Indians that I made up my mind I would never tell them any different.

INDEX

acorn 122
   See also: food; structures
adornment
   body paint 83, 115
   ear & nose piercing 54, 115
   feathers 113
   hair 91, 112, 113, 115, 117;
    facial hair 114
   headbands 113
   tattooing 54, 115
   See also: beads
antelope 35, 77, 109
   See also: hunting
arithmetic .... *See* counting
arrows 47, 51, 57, 79, 81, 82
   See also: bows; hunting
asphaltum 82, 83

badgers 35, 77
bags 65, 84
baskets 60, 64, 65, 66, 90
   See also: cradles; fishing; food
   preparation; hunting
bathing 38, 62, 68, 79, 88, 90
   See also: sweating
bats 77
beads 47, 115
Bear State Books 13
bears 35, 61, 76-77
beavers 77
Bellah, Mr. 21
blackbirds 36, 75
blankets 61, 70, 90, 99-100
blue birds 75
blue jays 75
bows 40, 46-47, 121
   See also: arrows; hunting; music
breechcloth 112
   See also: clothing
brushes 64, 114-115
buckeye 66
bulbs (food) 67
burial practices 91
buzzards 75

calls .... *See hunting*
Camp Babbitt 122
Campbell, William 120

Cape Horn 26
Cassidy's Ford 37
Centerville 41, 60, 97, 106, 120
chiefs .... *See* leadership
child care 89-90
chipmunks 77
Civil War 122
clothing 64, 70, 88, 90,
   100, 105, 112
clover 66, 68
Coalinga 82
colors 83
condors 75
cooking .... *See* food preparation
counting 53-54
coyotes 49, 50, 67
cradles 89-90, 100, 114
cranes 35-36, 75
crows 76
Cutler, Mrs. John 19

Davis, William Hawley 12-13
deer 49, 55, 56, 65, 76
   See also: hunting
dice 57, 66
directions 51
disease 110
doctors 50, 76, 83, 91, 113-114
dogs 76
Doniphan, Alexander W. 26
drugs 106
ducks 49, 75
   See also: hunting
Ducor 19
dummy ducks 55, 101
Dumna 40, 43

eagles 75-76, 113
eclipses 50
eels 76
elk 35, 65, 77, 109
   See also: hunting

falcons 83
family (size) 74
fighting 46, 55, 82, 87, 109;
   Indian/Anglo conficts 102-103,
   110, 117-121
fishing 50, 71-73, 76, 94, 97-99

food ....
   meals ....
   preparation 51, 61,
   86, 97, 98, 114
   storage ....
   See also: bags; baskets; hu
   fishing; structures
football ....
Fort Miller ....
foxes 77,
Fremont, John C. ....
Fremont Mines ...... *See* Las Mari

games 55-5
gaming courts ....
garbage ....
geese 49,
   See also: brushes; hunting
gender
   division of labor ....
   transsexuality ....
Ghee-gório ....
gigs .... *See* fi
Gilroy, John ....
gold .... *See* m
Gordon, Jack 12
gourds ....
grass nuts ....
greens (food) ....
guessing games ....
gum (chewing gum) ....
guns 4
Guthrie, John ....

handgame ....
Harrington, John P. ....
hawks 50,
hemp ....
hogs 12
hoop and pole games ....
horses ....
houses .... *See* struc
Houston, Sam ....
hunting
   (with) bow & arrows 7
   98, 100
   calls ....
   (with) nets 75, 9

124

from) rafts 97-98
with) smoke 73-74
with) snares & traps 46, 74, 75, 83-86, 98
talking 79, 80-81
with) throwing sticks 99
See also: arrows; bows
ation (boys') 88, 106
ws 60
kson, Andrew 25
son weed 106
gsburg 95
ship words 53
es 51
nance 40
táh-mah 60
guage 11, 12, 16, 49-54, 60, 95, 105
Mariposas 27, 37
a, Frank F. 9, 11-14, 19-22
lership 11, 87-88
or 87, 106, 109
n, Mr. & Mrs. 103
ners 91, 105, 106
nzanita 66, 106
riage 59-60, 110
son-Henry gang 122
s (tule) 61, 95, 96
licine men .... See doctors
ced River 36
kweed 64, 71, 84, 86, 90, 96-97, 99
erton 40, 60
er's lettuce 68
ing 27, 37, 40
See also: Las Mariposas
k 77
sion de San Jose [Mission Santa Clara?] 28
chell, Mike 19, 20, 21, 122
chila saddle 28
nache 15, 44, 46, 47, 109, 117-121
no (tribe) 15
on 50
rality 105-108, 109
rtars and pestles 59, 63, 64, 65, 66, 95, 111
untain lions 52, 70, 77, 79

mourning 91, 115
mud hens 75
music 69-70
mustard 68
nets .... See fishing; hunting
oats, wild 63
obsidian 81, 82, 83
Owens Lake 69
owls 49
Pacheco Creek 29
Pacheco Pass 29, 31
Paiutes 69
Patterson, John A. 120
peesh 77
pets 76
pigeons 83-86
pine nuts 67-68
pipes 59
population 110
porcupines 77
prostitution 107, 108
quail 69, 74
quivers 79
rabbits 77, 99
See also: blankets; clothing; hunting
raccoons 77
rafts 93-94, 97-98, 101, 111
reservations 101, 102, 109
rice (wild) 85
salt 68-69
salt grass 68
San Francisco ...... See Yerba Buena
San Joaquin Primeval 12
San Joaquin River 29, 32, 33, 36, 37, 40-41
San Jose (Pueblo de) 28
San Luis Gonzaga Creek 29, 32, 33
San Luis Obispo 121
San Luis Ranch 29, 33
seasons 50
seeds (food) 63
shinny 58
skunks 75
slings 55
smoking 59
snares .... See fishing; hunting
soaproot 64, 114

songs .... See music
spears .... See fishing
squirrels 35, 49, 64, 69, 73-74, 77
See also: hunting
story telling 69
string .... See hemp; milkweed
structures
    acorn granaries 63-64
    blinds 84
    fishing platforms 73
    houses .. 33, 42, 60-61, 95-96, 110
    shade 96
    sweat houses 61, 68, 80
sweating 79, 80, 110
See also structures
swimming 39, 40, 89
Tache 44, 60, 93
Tailholt (White River) 10, 20, 21
Tailholt Tales 13, 14
Telumne 44
Tivy, Captain 21
tobacco 59, 106
trade (between tribes) 44, 69
traps .... See fishing; hunting
travel 93-95, 111
Tripletts' Store 19
tule roots (food) 66-67
tules 36 64
See also: mats; rafts; structures; tule roots
Uncle Jeff's Story 12, 13, 14
Venice Hill 105
Visalia 19, 122, 123
Wah-táwk-ka 60
water pollution 68
water tag 105
whistling 70
White River (Tailholt) 10, 20, 21
wild flowers 33-34, 50, 67
wolves 77
wormwood 91
wrestling 55
Wukchumne 44, 60
Yerba Buena 27
Yoimut 16
Yokuts (definition) 11
Yosemite National Park
    Research Library 12
Zumwalt, M.C. 19

GREAT
VALLEY

Great Valley Books is an imprint of Heyday Books, Berkeley, California. Created in 2002 with a grant from The James Irvine Foundation and with the support of the Great Valley Center (Modesto, California), it strives to promote the rich literary, artistic, and cultural resources of California's Central Valley by publishing books of the highest merit and broadest interest.

Great Valley Books and other Central Valley titles published by Heyday Books:

Workin' Man Blues: Country Music in California,
by Gerald Haslam, with Alexandra Haslam Russell, and Richard Chon

Haslam's Valley, by Gerald Haslam

Peace Is a Four-Letter Word, by Janet Nichols Lynch

*Magpies and Mayflies: An Introduction to Plants and Animals
of the Central Valley and the Sierra Foothills,*
by Derek Madden, Ken Charters, and Cathy Snyder

Lion Singer, by Sylvia Ross

Dream Songs and Ceremony: Reflections on Traditional California Indian Dance,
by Frank LaPena

Walking the Flatlands: The Rural Landscape of the Lower Sacramento Valley,
by Mike Madison

Two-Hearted Oak: The Photography of Roman Loranc,
with text by Lillian Vallee

Bloodvine, by Aris Janigian

Structures of Utility, by David Stark Wilson

*Highway 99: A Literary Journey through California's
Great Central Valley,* edited by Stan Yogi

How Much Earth: The Fresno Poets,
edited by Christopher Buckley, David Oliveira, and M. L. Williams

Picturing California's Other Landscape,
edited by Heath Schenker

Henry Sugimoto: Painting an American Experience, by Kristine Kim

Bitter Melon: Inside America's Last Rural Chinese Town,
by Jeff Gillenkirk and James Motlow

HEYDAY INSTITUTE

Since its founding in 1974, Heyday Books has occupied a unique niche in the publishing world, specializing in books that foster an understanding of California history, literature, art, environment, social issues, and culture. We are a 501(c)(3) nonprofit organization based in Berkeley, California, serving a wide range of people and audiences throughout California and beyond. Our commitment is to enhance California's rich cultural heritage by providing a platform for writers, poets, artists, scholars, and storytellers who help keep this diverse legacy alive.

We are grateful for the generous funding we've received for our publications and programs during the past year from foundations and more than 300 individuals. Major recent supporters include:

Anonymous; Arroyo Fund; Bay Tree Fund; California Association of Resource Conservation Districts; California Oak Foundation; Candelaria Fund; CANfit; Columbia Foundation; Flow Fund Circle; Wallace Alexander Gerbode Foundation; Richard and Rhoda Goldman Fund; Evelyn & Walter Haas, Jr. Fund; Walter & Elise Haas Fund; James Irvine Foundation; Jeff Lustig; George Fredrick Jewett Foundation; LEF Foundation; James McClatchy; Michael McCone; Gordon and Betty Moore Foundation; National Endowment for the Arts; National Park Service; Alan Rosenus; John-Austin Saviano/Moore Foundation; LJ and Mary Skaggs Foundation; Strong Foundation for Environmental Values; Swinerton Family Fund; and the Harold and Alma White Memorial Fund.

For more information about Heyday Institute, our publications and programs, please visit our website at www.heydaybooks.com.